the ESSENTIAL
Canadian
Christmas
COOKBOOK

Lovoni Walker

Photographs by Merle Prosofsky

Lone Pine Publishing

The Publisher: Lone Pine Publishing

10145 – 81 Avenue
Edmonton, AB T6E 1W9
Canada

1808 – B Street NW, Suite 140
Auburn, WA 98001
USA

Website: www.lonepinepublishing.com

Library and Archives Canada Cataloguing in Publication

Walker, Lovoni, 1965–
     The essential Canadian Christmas cookbook / Lovoni Walker; photographs
     by Merle Prosofsky.

     Includes index.
     ISBN 1-55105-446-9

     1. Christmas cookery. I. Prosofsky, Merle, 1955– II. Title.
TX739.2.C45W34 2004   641.5'68   C2004-903910-5

Editorial Director: Nancy Foulds
Project Editor: Shelagh Kubish
Editorial: Shelagh Kubish, Rachelle Delaney, Lee Craig
Production Manager: Gene Longson
Book Design, Layout & Production: Elliot Engley
Cover Design: Elliot Engley
Cover Photo: Merle Prosofsky (Christmas sugar cookies)
Scanning, Separations & Film: Elite Lithographers Co.

Prop Stylist: Snez Ferenac
Thank you to the following merchants who allowed us to use props for our photo shoots: The Bay, Southgate; Stokes; Pier 1 Imports; Mikasa Home Store; Dansk Gifts.

We acknowledge the financial support of the Government of Canada through the Book Publishing Industry Development Program (BPIDP) for our publishing activities.

PC: 1

Contents

Introduction

Cooking is such an integral part of our daily lives, no time more so than at Christmas. All the baking, roasting, chopping, mixing and love that goes into the food we prepare during the holiday season is filled with tradition, but we also want to explore some new avenues and perhaps start some new traditions of our own.

Some of our most special memories center on the food of the holiday season. Warm spice fragrance fills the air, butter and sugar are being creamed in the mixer, a new batch of cookies sits waiting to be baked, while another sits cooling, ready to be decorated and transformed. Friends and family come around to share this special time of year, eagerly waiting to see what tempting morsels will be laid out for them.

Each year it seems the holiday season rolls around faster than the one before and each year we all vow to be better organized this time—to have the shopping, the baking and the card writing all done in advance. Sometimes, though, the most well-organized strategies don't happen as we plan.

During this busy time it will be a comfort to have a cookbook filled with all your favorite things to cook for the holiday season. You don't have to go searching through pages of books and magazines to find your favorite recipes—from truffles and cookies for gifts to the perfect roasted turkey, the delicious recipes are all right here in one book.

At the end of most of the recipes you will find handy make-ahead tips, including freezing and reheating tips where appropriate. There are plenty of hints to help you plan ahead for your festive season celebrations.

Of course we've included recipes for cooking the perfect Christmas Day meal, but we have also extended beyond that day. We have recipes for appetizers for pre-Christmas parties or special meals you can have cooking in the oven while you are out hanging pretty lights, decorating the trees or playing in the snow…hearty, wholesome recipes to warm you and chase away the winter chills. Also included is a selection of party drinks and desserts that will tempt any soul.

Christmas is a time to reflect upon who and what is important in our lives. It's a time to embrace the spirit that is Christmas and to enjoy happy moments with family and friends. Make your festive cooking an enjoyable experience—cook with love, fill your house with delicious aromas, drink it all in and make this Christmas an extra special one.

May the Christmas Season be a joyous one for all of you. Happy Cooking!

In Our Kitchen

Here is some useful information about the ingredients, cooking terms and techniques we use in our recipes.

Ingredients

Milk is whole milk (homo, 3.25%MF).

Eggs are large size.

Butter is salted.

We use freshly ground pepper for the best, most intense flavor.

Mushrooms are small to medium white or brown unless otherwise specified.

Broth (stock) is bought prepared in a Tetra Pak or is homemade or, in a pinch, you can make it from bouillon powder mixed with water according to directions on the package.

Wines and sherry used are alcoholic. Substitute chicken broth (in savory recipes) if you prefer, but the flavor will differ from the original recipe.

Citrus juices such as lemon, orange and lime are fresh.

Unless otherwise specified, olive oil is extra virgin.

Measuring

Measure dry and semi-solid ingredients in dry-measure cups and level off using straight edge of the back of a knife.

Measure liquids in glass or plastic liquid measures.

This book uses both imperial and metric measurements where appropriate. For items measured by weight, we have given the metric equivalent in grams, not milliliters.

As most packaged dry goods indicate their weight in grams whether in bulk or on the package, our approach should make it easier for you to find and measure the correct quantity.

Baking dishes

To measure the capacity of a baking dish, fill it with water and then pour the water into a large measuring jug. The following measurement conversions are approximate and have been scaled either up or down.

4 cups/1 qt/1 liter

6 cups/1½ qt/1.5 liters

8 cups/2 qt/2 liters

10 cups/2½ qt/2.5 liters

12 cups/3 qt/3 liters

Breadcrumbs

To make fresh breadcrumbs, place day-old bread in food processor and process until fine (or coarse) crumbs. Breadcrumbs can be stored in 1 cup (or greater quantities) in small freezer bags, sealed and placed in freezer and thawed as needed.

Melting chocolate

Method 1—Place chocolate in small microwave-safe bowl. Do not cover. Microwave on 70% power in 40-second intervals until almost melted. Stir until smooth and chocolate is completely melted.

* Please note, although every endeavor has been made to print accurate recipes, cooking times in the book are approximate. Cooking times can vary according to different ovens and the type of cookware you use.

Method 2—Place chocolate in medium stainless or heatproof glass bowl. Place bowl over small saucepan of simmering (not boiling) water, ensuring bowl is not sitting in water. Stir for 2 to 3 minutes or until chocolate is almost melted. Remove bowl from heat and continue to stir until smooth and chocolate is completely melted.

Toasting coconut and nuts

To toast coconut or nuts, place on baking sheet and toast in 350°F (180°C) oven for 5 to 8 minutes, stirring occasionally, until golden brown. Times will vary according to different ovens.

To toast a small amount, place in small frying pan and toast over medium heat, stirring constantly, for about 3 to 7 minutes, until golden brown.

Bruising cardamom pods

Place a pod on a cutting board and press down firmly using the flat side of a knife, the bottom of a saucepan or a meat mallet until pod opens slightly.

Almond Crisps with Port and Cranberry Chutney

The sweetness of the chutney makes a perfect partner with a creamy cheese such as Cambozola or Brie. The recipe is completely make-ahead, but remember to take the cheese and chutney out of the refrigerator 1 hour before serving to allow them to soften.

Almond Crisps

- 2 egg whites
- 1/3 cup granulated sugar
- 1 cup all purpose flour
- 1/2 tsp coarsely ground pepper
- 1/4 tsp ground cinnamon
- 1/4 tsp ground nutmeg
- 1/4 tsp salt
- 1 cup (5 oz/155 g) whole almonds

Port and Cranberry Chutney

- 3 cups port
- 1 1/2 cups (5 1/2 oz/170 g) dried cranberries, coarsely chopped
- 1/4 cup packed brown sugar
- 2 tsp balsamic vinegar
- 1/4 tsp salt

Grease an 8 x 4 x 2 inch (20 x 10 x 5 cm) loaf pan. Preheat oven to 325°F (160°C).

Almond Crisps: Beat egg whites and sugar in medium bowl, using electric mixer, for about 3 minutes or until mixture is white and thick.

Stir in flour, spices and salt; mix well. Spoon into prepared pan and smooth top. Bake in preheated oven for about 35 minutes or until lightly browned around edges; cool in pan for 1 hour.

Turn out onto cutting board and cut into 1/8 inch (3 mm) thick slices. Place slices in single layer on non-greased baking sheets. Bake in preheated oven for about 15 minutes or until crisp and lightly golden; cool completely before storing.

Cambozola is a mild, creamy blue cheese. You can also use an aged white cheddar, strong blue cheese or creamy Camembert.

Port and Cranberry Chutney: Combine port, cranberries, sugar, vinegar and salt in medium saucepan and stir over medium heat until sugar is dissolved. Boil gently for about 15 minutes, stirring occasionally, or until thickened. Chutney will continue to thicken as it cools.

Do-ahead tips: Crisps can be made 4 days ahead and stored in a sealed container in a cool place. The chutney can be made a week ahead and stored in a sealed container in the refrigerator.

Seafood Pouches with Lime Dipping Sauce

These tasty little morsels can either be deep-fried or steamed in a large bamboo steamer. Steamers are available from Asian grocery stores. Serve hot.

Seafood Pouches

- 1 Tbsp canola oil
- ¼ cup thinly sliced green onions
- 2 garlic cloves, minced
- 1 tsp thinly grated gingerroot
- ¼ cup grated carrot
- 11 oz (340 g) bag medium raw shrimp, peeled, finely chopped
- 11 oz (340 g) bag scallops
- 2 Tbsp finely chopped fresh cilantro
- 1½ Tbsp soy sauce
- 1 Tbsp Thai sweet chili sauce
- 1 lb (500 g) package round Shanghai dumpling wrappers (about 60 to 65), thawed if frozen

canola oil for deep-frying

Lime Dipping Sauce

- ¼ cup lime juice
- 3 Tbsp Thai sweet chili sauce
- 2 tsp soy sauce
- 1 tsp sesame oil
- 1 tsp fish sauce

Seafood Pouches:
Combine oil, onion, garlic, ginger and carrot in small frying pan over medium-high heat. Cook for about 2 minutes or until fragrant; spoon into medium bowl.

Add shrimp, scallops, cilantro, soy sauce and chili sauce and stir until well combined.

Spoon a rounded teaspoon of mixture into center of each dumpling wrapper. Lightly brush a little water around edge of wrapper. Bring wrapper up around filling and press to seal. Keep covered with tea towel to prevent drying out. Repeat with remaining filling and wrappers.

Deep-fried Variation: Heat oil to 350°F (180°C). Cook pouches, in batches, for about 2 minutes or until golden brown and cooked through; drain on paper towel.

Steamed Variation: Place half of the pouches in single layers in a large, greased bamboo steamer basket—this recipe was tested in a two-tiered steamer. Ensure pouches are not touching each other. Place steamer basket over large pot or Dutch oven of boiling water. Steamer should fit snugly into the top of the pot so very little steam escapes. Cover tightly and cook for about 15 minutes or until wrappers are tender and seafood is cooked. Repeat with remaining pouches.

Lime Dipping Sauce: Combine all ingredients in a small bowl.

Do-ahead tips: *These pouches can be made a day ahead. Store on parchment paper–lined baking sheets and cover with plastic wrap. Freeze them and then transfer frozen pouches to a sealed container or resealable plastic bags for up to 1 month. Thaw, covered, in single layer, on parchment paper–lined baking sheets before cooking.*

Antipasto Platter

This appetizer does require a little extra time for grilling the vegetables, but it is the perfect do-ahead appetizer—all you have to do when guests arrive is toast the bread. You can add store-bought marinated artichokes and mushrooms to the platter along with a selection of deli meats. Remove grilled vegetables from the refrigerator 1 hour before serving. Vegetables can be cooked on a barbecue, electric grill or grill pan.

Slow Roasted Tomatoes

12 ripe medium Roma tomatoes, halved lengthwise

2 tsp granulated sugar

salt and pepper to sprinkle

Grilled Vegetables

1½ lb (750 g) yam (orange sweet potato), peeled and cut lengthwise into ¼ inch (6 mm) thick slices

1 medium eggplant, cut lengthwise into ¼ inch (6 mm) thick slices

2 medium zucchini, cut lengthwise into ¼ inch (6 mm) thick slices

2 large red peppers, quartered, seeds and membranes removed

¼ cup olive oil

Balsamic Marinade

¾ cup olive oil

⅓ cup balsamic vinegar

¼ cup finely grated fresh Parmesan cheese

2 Tbsp chopped fresh oregano

2 Tbsp Thai sweet chili sauce

2 garlic cloves, minced

1 tsp packed brown sugar

¼ tsp salt

¼ tsp coarsely ground pepper

Toasts

1 to 2 loaves crusty bread such as ciabatta

3 Tbsp olive oil

2 garlic cloves, halved

Slow Roasted Tomatoes: Grease wire rack and place on baking sheet. Preheat oven to 250°F (120°C).

Place tomatoes, cut side up, on wire rack. Sprinkle with sugar, salt and pepper. Roast in preheated oven for about 4 hours or until semi-dried. Let cool, then transfer to large container with sealed lid.

Grilled Vegetables: Grease grill and preheat to medium heat. Brush both sides of yam, eggplant and zucchini lightly with oil. Cook on preheated grill for 3 to 8 minutes each side until softened and grill marks appear; place in container with tomatoes. Set aside.

Cook peppers, skin side down, on grill, until skin blackens and blisters. Or broil peppers in oven, skin side up. Place roasted peppers in small bowl and cover with plastic wrap; let cool for 10 minutes. Peel and chop peppers into ⅓ inch (1 cm) thick strips; add to other vegetables.

Drizzle vegetables with Balsamic Marinade and toss to coat. Seal and refrigerate for 8 hours or overnight.

Balsamic Marinade: Place all ingredients in jar and shake well to combine.

Toasts: Preheat oven to 350°F (180°C). Cut bread into ⅓ inch (1 cm) thick slices, and brush both sides of each slice lightly with oil. Arrange in single layer on baking sheet. Toast in preheated oven for about 10 minutes, turning once, until lightly golden. Rub garlic clove over one side of each piece of bread. Serve bread with the antipasto platter.

Do-ahead tips: *The vegetables can be made 3 days ahead and stored in a sealed container in the refrigerator. Turn container several times to allow all vegetables to be evenly coated in marinade.*

Creamy Mushroom Soup

Dried mushrooms give the soup a deep, earthy flavor. They are available in most grocery stores or specialty food stores.

¾ oz (22 g) package dried exotic mushrooms

2 Tbsp butter

1 Tbsp olive oil

2 lbs (1 kg) brown or white mushrooms, thinly sliced (about 10 cups)

1 cup sliced green onions

4 cloves garlic, minced

⅓ cup dry sherry

¼ cup all purpose flour

¼ tsp salt

¼ tsp coarsely ground pepper

4 cups chicken broth

¾ cup whipping cream

Place dried mushrooms in small heatproof bowl and cover with warm water. Let stand for 20 minutes; drain. Coarsely chop, discarding any tough stalks; set aside.

Heat butter and oil in large pot or Dutch oven over medium heat. Add fresh mushrooms, onion and garlic and cook, stirring occasionally, for about 10 minutes or until softened.

Stir in sherry, flour, salt and pepper. Cook, stirring, for 1 minute.

Gradually stir in broth and reconstituted mushrooms. Increase heat to high and bring to boil, then reduce heat to low. Simmer, covered, for about 20 minutes or until slightly thickened; cool slightly.

Remove 2 cups of mixture and set aside. Process remaining mixture in blender in 2 or 3 batches until smooth. Return mixture to same pot.

Add cream and reserved mushroom mixture and stir over medium heat until hot.

Spicy Nut Nibble Mix

You can use one or a selection of your favorite nuts for this recipe. The recipe can easily be doubled or tripled if you want to give some away as gifts.

1 egg white

1 tsp cayenne pepper

1 tsp ground cumin

½ tsp salt

½ tsp coarsely ground pepper

¼ tsp ground cinnamon

⅓ cup granulated sugar

1 cup (5 oz/155 g) cashews

1 cup (5 oz/155 g) whole almonds

1 cup (4 oz/125 g) pecans

Line a baking sheet with parchment paper. Preheat oven to 375°F (190°C).

Whisk egg white, cayenne pepper, cumin, salt, pepper, cinnamon and sugar in large bowl.

Add nuts and stir to coat. Spread mixture on prepared baking sheet. Cook in preheated oven, stirring occasionally, for about 30 minutes or until nuts are golden. Mixture will become crisp as the nuts cool. Cool completely before storing.

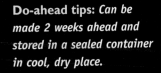

Do-ahead tips: *Can be made 2 weeks ahead and stored in a sealed container in cool, dry place.*

Sweet Chili Chicken Skewers with Lime Aioli

These are equally delicious served with Thai sweet chili sauce for dipping if you don't want to make the Lime Aioli for dipping.

Sweet Chili Chicken

- ¼ cup Thai sweet chili sauce
- ¼ cup lime juice
- 3 Tbsp light olive oil
- 3 Tbsp chopped fresh cilantro
- 1 Tbsp soy sauce
- ¼ tsp coarsely ground pepper
- 5 boneless, skinless chicken breasts
- 40 wooden 8 inch (20 cm) skewers, soaked in water

Lime Aioli

- 2 egg yolks
- 3 garlic cloves, minced
- 2 Tbsp lime juice
- pinch of salt
- 1 cup light olive oil
- 2 Tbsp Thai sweet chili sauce

Sweet Chili Chicken: Combine chili sauce, juice, oil, cilantro, soy sauce and pepper in large bowl.

Remove tenderloin from underside of each chicken breast and cut tenderloins in half lengthwise; add to marinade. Cut each chicken breast diagonally crosswise into thin slices. Add to marinade and toss to coat. Cover and refrigerate for 3 hours.

Drain and thread one piece of chicken lengthwise onto each skewer.

Heat grill pan (such as cast iron grill, barbecue or electric grill) over medium-high heat. Brush with oil. Cook chicken in 2 to 3 batches for about 3 minutes each side until tender. Remove and cover with foil to keep warm while cooking remaining skewers.

Lime Aioli: Whisk yolks, garlic, juice and salt in medium bowl until well combined. Place bowl over small saucepan of simmering water, ensuring bottom of bowl is not sitting in water. Add oil in thin steady stream, whisking constantly until mixture is thick and pale. This process should take about 10 minutes. Stir in sauce.

Or, place yolks, garlic, juice and salt in food processor. Process until well combined and pale. With motor running, drizzle oil through feed chute in thin steady stream until thick. Add sauce and process until well combined. This method takes 3 to 4 minutes.

Do-ahead tips: *Lime Aioli can be made 3 days ahead and stored in a sealed container in refrigerator. Marinade can be made 3 days ahead and stored in a sealed container in refrigerator. Marinate chicken up to 3 hours ahead.*

Cheese Quesadillas with Lime Peach Salsa

Quesadilla wedges are best served hot while they are still crisp with the cheese melting. To keep them warm while you are cooking the remaining ones, put them on a wire rack on a baking sheet and place, uncovered, in a warm oven (200°F/120°C).

Cheese Quesadillas

- 2 cups grated Monterey jalapeno cheese
- ½ cup sour cream
- 6 large flour tortillas

Lime Peach Salsa

- 14 fl oz (398 ml) can peach halves in natural juice, drained, finely chopped
- 2 ripe medium tomatoes, quartered, seeded, finely chopped
- ⅓ cup finely chopped red onion
- 2 garlic cloves, minced
- 2 Tbsp finely chopped fresh cilantro
- 2 Tbsp lime juice
- 1 tsp pepper sauce
- ¼ tsp salt

Cheese Quesadillas: Combine cheese and sour cream in small bowl. Spread half of one side of each tortilla with cheese mixture. Fold other half over to cover filling. Press down lightly to seal.

Heat large frying pan over medium heat until hot. Cook quesadillas for 2 to 3 minutes each side until golden brown and crisp. Cut each into 6 wedges. Serve with Lime and Peach Salsa.

Lime Peach Salsa: Combine all ingredients in medium bowl. Serve immediately or cover and chill for 1 to 3 hours before serving to allow flavor to develop.

Do-ahead tips:
Quesadillas can be made a day ahead and stored, wrapped, in plastic wrap in the refrigerator. They can be frozen for 1 month and thawed in refrigerator before cooking.

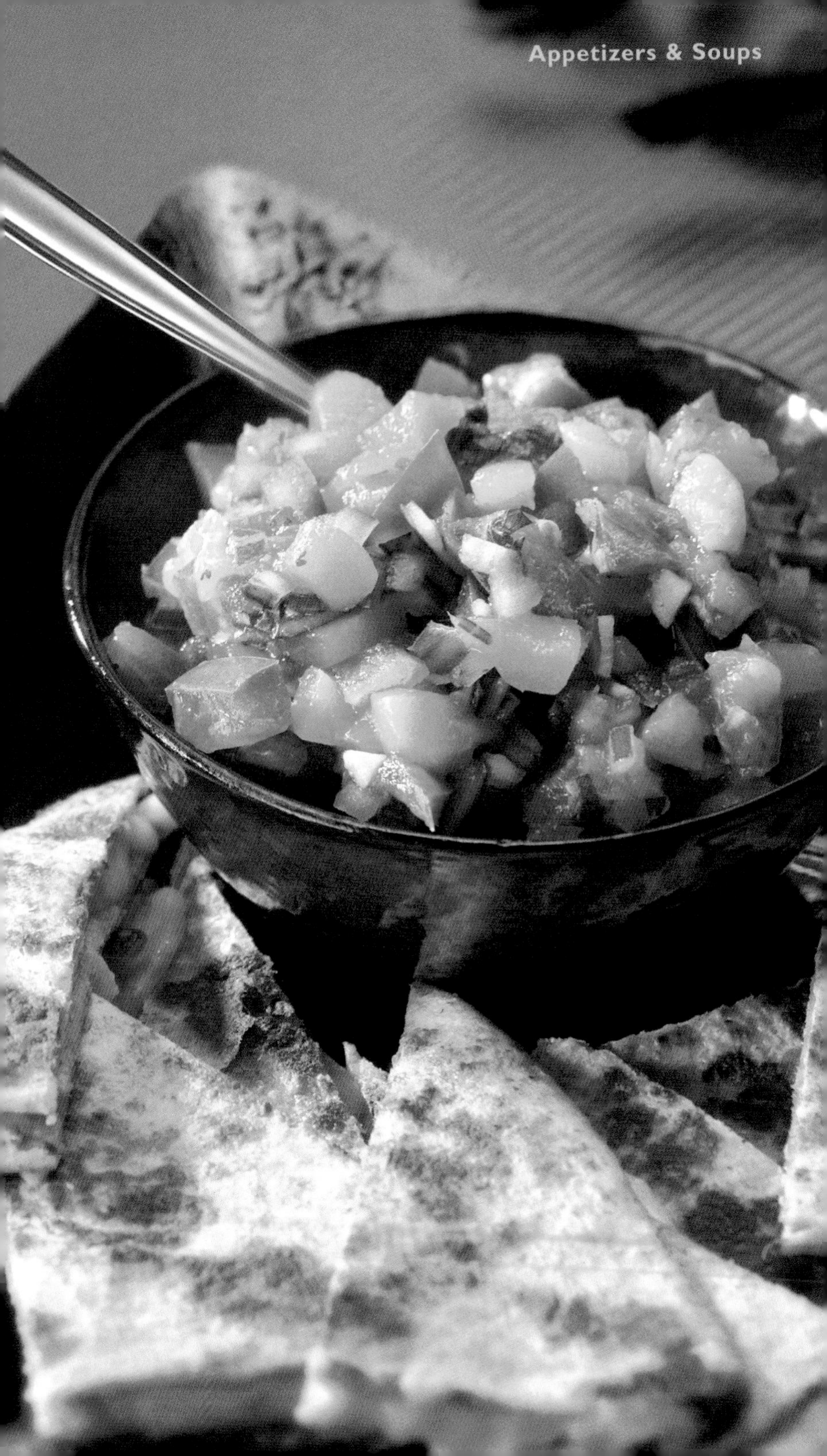

Spicy Antipasto

Antipasto makes a great gift—arrange a jar of it in a basket, add some delicious deli breads or crackers, some cheese and a bottle of wine and you have a perfect Christmas gift for a host, friend or neighbor.

14 fl oz (398 ml) can tomato sauce

14 fl oz (398 ml) can artichoke hearts, drained, chopped

10 fl oz (300 ml) jar pickled mushrooms, drained, chopped

1 cup red wine vinegar

1/2 cup packed brown sugar

2 cups chopped cauliflower florets

1 cup chopped pickled onions

1/2 cup stuffed green olives, thinly sliced

1/3 cup pitted kalamata olives, thinly sliced

2 cups chopped red peppers

1 Tbsp pepper sauce

2 tsp crushed dried chilies

1/4 tsp salt

1/2 tsp coarsely ground pepper

4 garlic cloves, minced

2 cans (6 oz/170 g) tuna packed in spring water, flaked

1/4 cup chopped fresh basil

Combine all ingredients except tuna and basil in large pot or Dutch oven. Bring to boil then reduce heat to medium-low. Simmer, uncovered, stirring occasionally, for about 20 minutes or until thickened.

Stir in tuna and basil. Spoon mixture into hot sterilized jars and seal.

Do-ahead tips: Mixture can be made 4 weeks ahead and stored in sealed containers in refrigerator. Once open, use within 1 week.

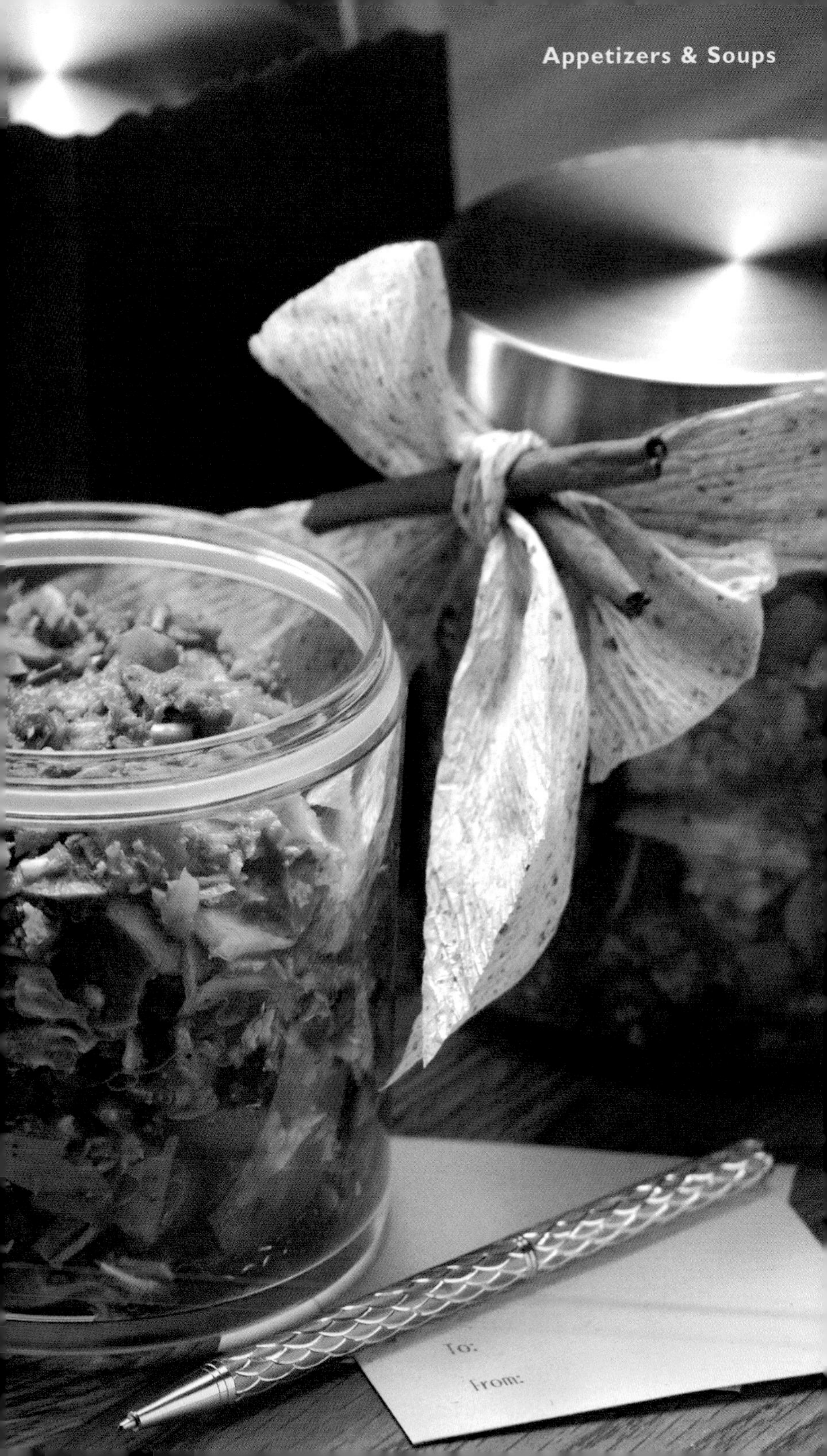
To:
From:

Sweet Meatballs with Yogurt Dipping Sauce

The meatballs can also be deep-fried in hot (350°F/180°C) oil until browned and cooked through.

Sweet Meatballs

- 1 Tbsp olive oil
- ½ cup finely chopped onion
- 2 cloves garlic, minced
- 1 tsp ground cumin
- ½ tsp coarsely ground pepper
- ¼ tsp ground cinnamon
- 1 lb (500 g) ground beef
- ½ cup fine dried breadcrumbs (see p. 6)
- 1 egg, lightly beaten
- ¼ cup (1½ oz/45 g) dried currants
- ⅓ cup (1½ oz/45 g) slivered almonds, toasted (see p. 7), finely chopped
- ¼ cup chopped fresh parsley
- 1 tsp finely grated orange rind

Yogurt Dipping Sauce

- ¾ cup plain yogurt
- 1 Tbsp liquid honey
- 1 Tbsp lemon juice
- ¼ tsp coarsely ground pepper
- pinch of salt

Sweet Meatballs: Line a baking sheet with parchment paper. Preheat oven to 350°F (180°C).

Heat oil in small frying pan over medium heat. Add onion and garlic and cook for about 5 minutes or until softened. Add cumin, pepper and cinnamon and cook for about 1 minute or until fragrant. Scrape into large bowl.

Do-ahead tips: *Meatballs can be prepared 2 days ahead and stored, covered, in refrigerator. If you want to freeze them, place on a baking sheet, cover with plastic wrap and freeze until solid. Once frozen, transfer to resealable freezer bags. Thaw completely in a single layer on a baking sheet before cooking.*

Add remaining ingredients and mix well to combine. Roll tablespoons of mixture into balls and place on prepared baking sheet. Cook in preheated oven, turning once during cooking, for about 20 minutes or until browned and cooked through.

Yogurt Dipping Sauce: Combine all ingredients in small bowl.

Artichoke and Cheese Dip

Use an assortment of sliced vegetables, tortilla crisps or torn pieces of crusty bread for dipping.

14 fl oz (398 ml) can artichokes, drained, chopped

1 cup grated white cheddar cheese

½ cup finely grated fresh Parmesan cheese

¼ cup sour cream

¼ cup mayonnaise

¼ cup thinly sliced green onions

¼ tsp paprika

Grease a 2 to 3 cup ovenproof serving dish. Preheat oven to 350°F (180°C).

Combine all ingredients except paprika in a medium bowl. Spread into prepared dish.

Sprinkle with paprika. Bake in preheated oven for about 20 minutes or until hot and bubbling around sides. Serve warm.

Do-ahead tips: *The dip can be prepared 1 or 2 days ahead, spread into an ovenproof serving dish, covered with plastic wrap and stored in refrigerator. Remove from refrigerator 30 minutes before baking.*

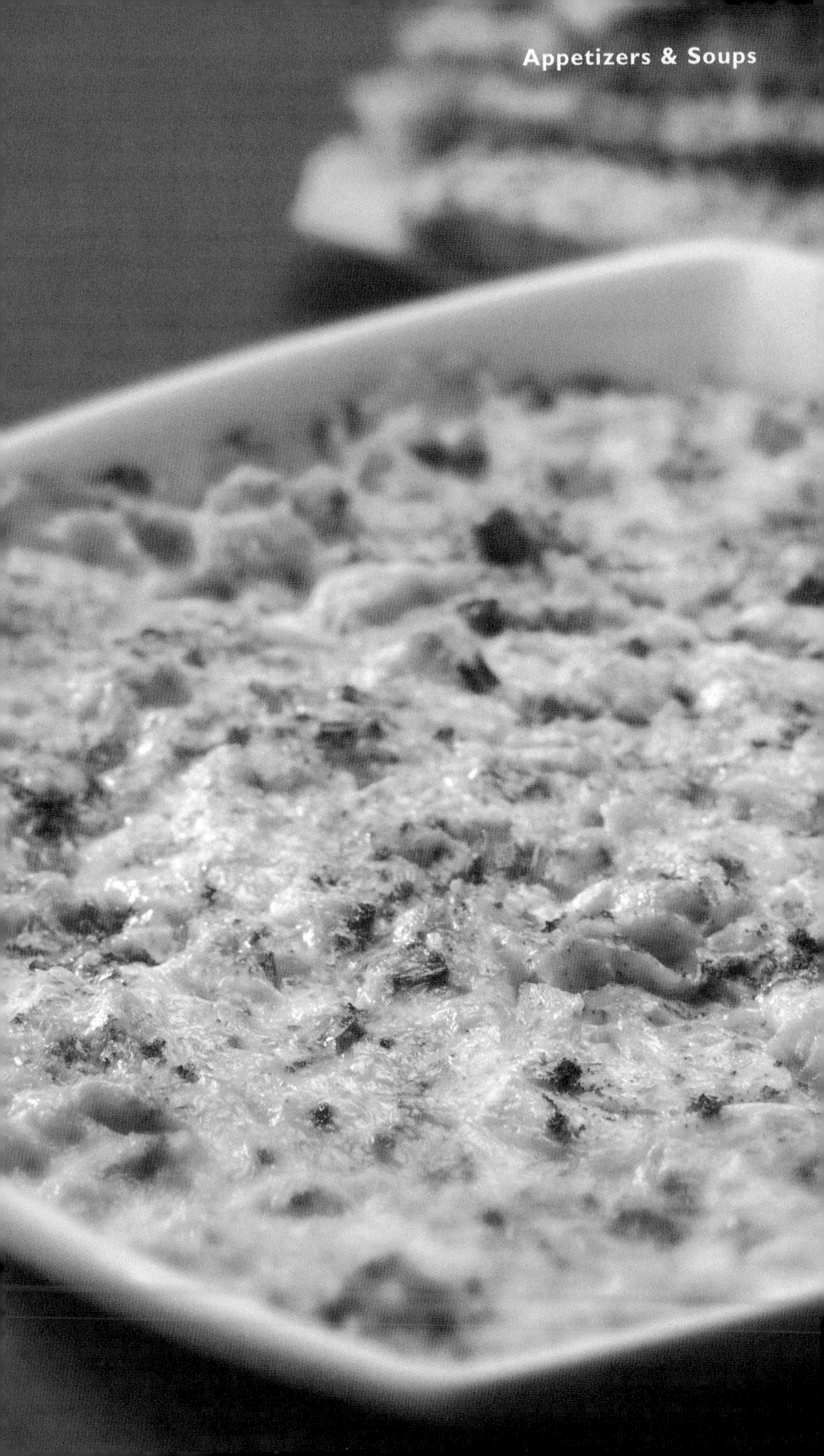

Mini Shrimp Rolls

You can substitute lobster or crab for the shrimp if preferred.

1 Tbsp butter

3 Tbsp dry sherry

1 lb (500 g) raw medium shrimp, peeled, deveined

1/3 cup finely chopped celery

1/3 cup finely chopped green onions

2 Tbsp mayonnaise

1 Tbsp lemon juice

1/4 tsp salt

15 dinner rolls

sprinkle cayenne pepper

Melt butter in large frying pan over medium heat. Add sherry and heat until bubbling.

Add shrimp and cook for about 2 minutes or until pink and just cooked; do not overcook. Chop shrimp and place in medium bowl; cool.

Add celery, onion, mayonnaise, juice and salt and stir until well combined.

Cut dinner rolls across the top and almost through to bottom taking care not to cut through. Spoon filling into each roll. Sprinkle with cayenne pepper.

Do-ahead tips: *The filling can be made a day ahead and stored in a sealed container in the refrigerator.*

Shrimp Cocktail with Avocado Sauce

Take a step back in time with a revamped version of an old favorite, a simple, fun and delicious way to start a meal. The avocado sauce is best made just before serving.

Shrimp Cocktail

- 11 oz (340 g) bag large raw shrimp, unpeeled
- 1/2 tsp salt
- 1 cup shredded romaine lettuce

Avocado Sauce

- 1 large ripe avocado, halved seed removed
- 2 Tbsp sour cream
- 1 1/2 Tbsp lime juice
- 1 Tbsp Thai sweet chili sauce
- 1/4 tsp salt

Shrimp Cocktail: Place shrimp in a large steamer in a large saucepan over simmering water; sprinkle with salt. Steam for 2 to 3 minutes or until pink and just cooked, do not overcook; cool.

Peel and devein shrimp, leaving tails intact.

Place a little shredded lettuce into bottom of four cocktail glasses. Arrange shrimp around edge of glass. Place a spoonful of Avocado Sauce in center.

Avocado Sauce: Mash avocado in small bowl until smooth. Add remaining ingredients and mix well.

Do-ahead tips:
Shrimp can be cooked and peeled 1 day ahead and stored in a sealed container in refrigerator.

Roasted Pepper Tarts

You can use chopped fresh basil instead of parsley if you prefer. These tarts are best served warm.

2 medium red peppers, quartered, seeds and membranes removed

1/2 cup half and half (10% MF)

3/4 cup sour cream

4 eggs

1/3 cup finely grated fresh Parmesan cheese

2 Tbsp chopped fresh parsley

1/4 tsp salt

1/4 tsp coarsely ground pepper

12 1/2 oz (397 g) package frozen puff pastry, thawed

Place peppers skin side up on baking sheet under hot broiler. Broil for about 5 minutes until skin is blistered and blackened. Place in small bowl, cover with plastic wrap and let stand for 10 minutes. Peel peppers and finely chop.

Lightly grease mini muffin pans. Preheat oven to 350°F (180°C).

Filling: Whisk half and half, sour cream, eggs, cheese, parsley, salt and pepper in medium bowl.

Roll half of pastry out on lightly floured surface until about 13 inch (32.5 cm) square. Using 3 inch (7.5 cm) round cutter, cut 16 circles from one pastry half. Press rounds into prepared muffin pans. Repeat with remaining pastry half.

Spoon about 1 teaspoon of roasted pepper into each pastry case. Spoon about 2 teaspoons of filling over pepper. Bake on bottom rack in preheated oven for 20 to 25 minutes or until filling is set and pastry is golden. Serve warm.

Do-ahead tips: *The filling can be prepared a day ahead and stored in a sealed container in refrigerator. The tarts can be baked 1 to 3 hours ahead of time and reheated on baking sheets for about 10 to 12 minutes before serving.*

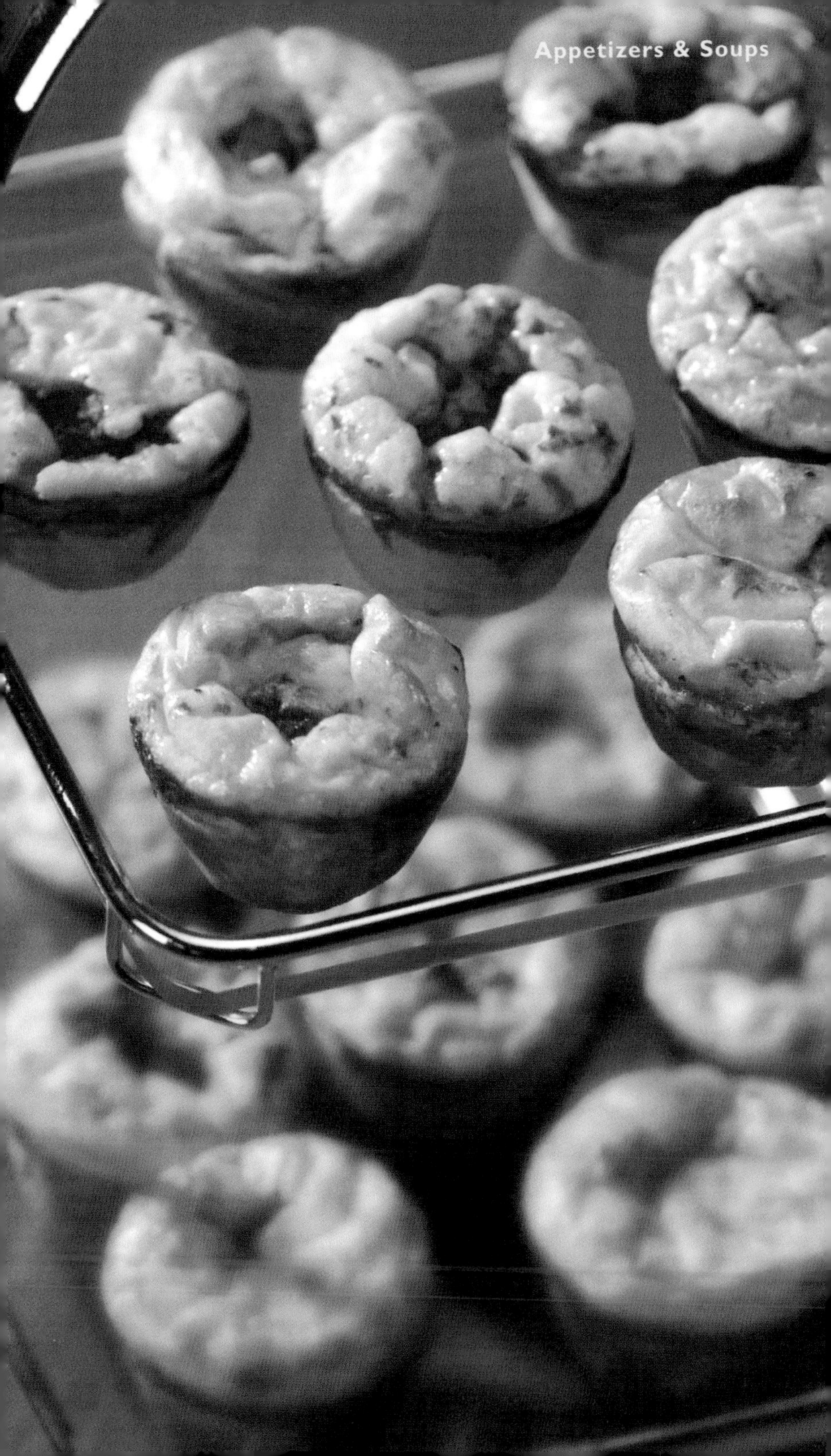

Seafood Soup

You can remove the cooked mussel meat from the shells before serving if desired. They make such a nice presentation that we preferred to serve them still in their shells. This hearty stew-like soup would also make a delicious light main meal served with crusty bread and a green salad.

| 1 Tbsp olive oil |
| 1 cup chopped onion |
| 1 cup finely chopped red pepper |
| 4 garlic cloves, minced |
| 1 cup dry white wine |
| 28 fl oz (789 ml) can diced tomatoes |
| 2 cups chicken broth |
| ¼ cup tomato paste |
| 1 tsp granulated sugar |
| ½ tsp salt |
| ½ tsp coarsely ground pepper |
| ¾ lb (375 g) cod or halibut, cut into ½ inch (1.2 cm) pieces |
| ½ lb (250 g) mussels, scrubbed clean if necessary |
| 11 oz (340 g) bag raw medium shrimp, peeled, deveined, halved crosswise |
| ½ lb (250 g) scallops |

Heat oil in large pot or Dutch oven over medium heat. Add onion and pepper and cook, stirring occasionally, for about 10 minutes or until softened. Add garlic and cook for about 3 minutes until softened and fragrant.

Add wine, tomatoes with their juice, broth, paste, sugar, salt and pepper. Bring to boil then reduce heat to medium-low. Simmer, uncovered, stirring occasionally, for 10 minutes.

Add cod and mussels; cover and cook for 3 minutes. Add shrimp and cook for 2 minutes. Gently stir in scallops and cook for 1 to 2 minutes or until just cooked.

French Onion Soup

Cooking the onion for a longer period of time sweetens it, mellowing its flavor.

1 Tbsp olive oil

6 cups packed thinly sliced onions

1 cup dry sherry

4 cups beef broth

1 bay leaf

1 sprig fresh thyme

salt and pepper to taste

3 cups cubed baguette in ¾ inch (2 cm) pieces

2 cups grated Gruyere cheese

Heat oil in large pot or Dutch oven over medium-low heat. Add onion and cook, covered, stirring occasionally, for about 45 minutes or until onion is very soft and brown.

Stir in sherry, broth, bay leaf and thyme. Cover and bring to boil. Reduce heat to low. Simmer, stirring occasionally, for 20 minutes to allow flavors to develop.

Remove bay leaf and thyme stalk. Season with salt and pepper. Pour into 4, 2 cup ovenproof dishes (or 6, 1½ cup dishes).

Top with bread then sprinkle with cheese. Place under hot broiler for 1 to 2 minutes until cheese is melted.

Do-ahead tips: *Soup can be made 1 to 2 days in advance and refrigerated in a sealed container. Reheat before spooning into serving dishes and topping with bread cubes and cheese.*

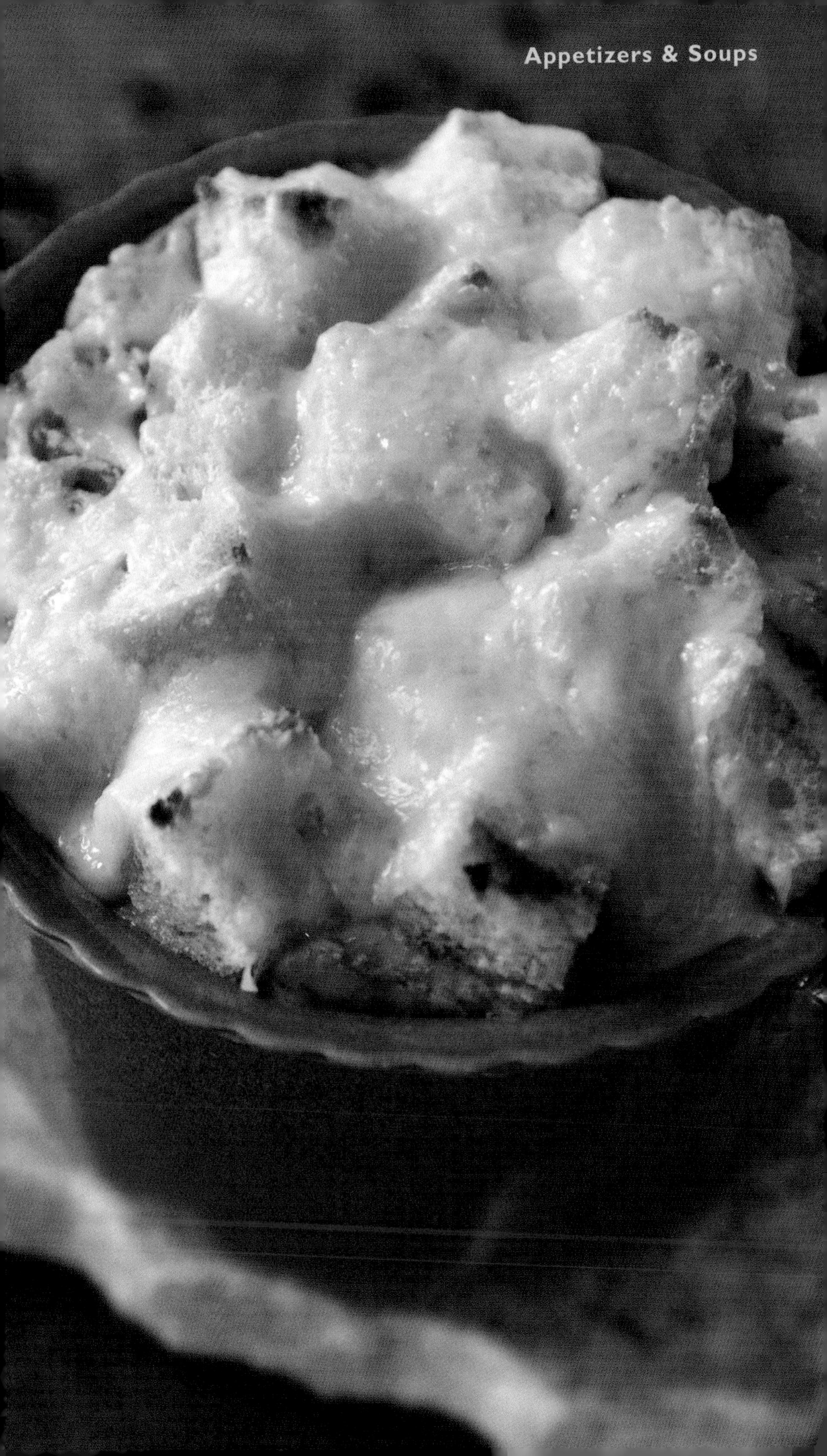

Creamy Roasted Yam Soup

This soup makes a perfect starter with thick, crusty bread for Christmas Day or cold wintery nights. Roasting the yams helps to caramelize them, sweetening their flavor.

3 lbs yams (sweet potatoes) peeled and cut into 1 inch (2.5 cm) cubes

1 Tbsp olive oil, plus another 1 Tbsp

1/2 tsp ground cumin

1/4 tsp salt

1/4 tsp coarsely ground pepper

1/4 tsp cayenne pepper

1 cup chopped onion

2 cloves garlic, minced

6 cups chicken broth

1 cup whipping cream

Grease a baking sheet. Preheat oven to 375°F (190°C).

Combine yam, 1 tablespoon of oil, cumin, salt, pepper and cayenne pepper on prepared baking sheet. Roast in preheated oven, stirring occasionally, for about 50 minutes or until softened and lightly browned.

Heat extra oil in large pot or Dutch oven over medium-high heat. Add onion and cook, stirring occasionally, for about 10 minutes or until onion is softened and browned (browning the onion helps to give the soup its flavor). Add garlic and cook for about 2 minutes until fragrant.

Add yam and broth and stir. Process in blender in 3 to 4 batches until smooth. Return mixture to same pot and bring to boil, then reduce to medium-low.

Add cream and stir until well combined and hot. Season with extra salt and pepper if desired.

Do-ahead tips: *Soup can be made 1 to 3 days ahead and stored in a sealed container in refrigerator. To reheat, place in a large pot or Dutch oven and stir over medium-low heat until hot.*

Herb Butter Turkey

Your Christmas feast will be a sure hit with this succulent turkey stuffed with pine nuts and dried apricots and served with cranberry gravy.

10 lb (4.5 kg) turkey
1/2 cup butter, softened
2 tsp chopped fresh thyme
1 tsp celery salt
1/4 tsp coarsely ground pepper
2 cloves garlic, minced

Cranberry Gravy
1/4 cup all purpose flour
1/4 cup brandy or chicken broth
3 cups chicken or turkey broth
1/2 cup cranberry jelly
salt and pepper to taste

Pine Nut and Apricot Stuffing
6 slices bacon, chopped
1 cup chopped onion
1/2 cup chopped celery
1/2 cup (2 1/2 oz/75 g) finely chopped dried apricots
1 loaf (20 oz/597 g) day-old bread, crusts removed, diced (about 6 cups)
1/2 cup (3 oz/90 g) pine nuts, toasted (see p. 7)
1/4 cup chopped fresh parsley
1/4 cup cranberry jelly
2 tsp finely grated orange rind
salt and pepper

Lightly grease wire rack and place inside roasting pan. Preheat oven to 350°F (180°C).

Remove and discard neck, giblets and any fat from turkey cavities. Rinse inside and out with cold water; pat dry with paper towel.

Combine butter, thyme, celery salt, pepper and garlic in small bowl. Using fingers, carefully loosen turkey skin across breast and legs to separate skin from meat, being careful not to pierce skin. Evenly spread butter mixture between skin and meat; smooth skin.

Tuck wings under body. Fill body and neck cavity with Pine Nut and Apricot Stuffing. Secure openings with toothpicks or skewers.

Do-ahead tips:
Stuffing can be made 1 month ahead and frozen in a sealed plastic bag or airtight container in freezer. Thaw stuffing before placing it into turkey. Stuff turkey just before cooking. Note that the stuffing does compact when frozen and thawed.

tie legs together. Place in prepared pan. Pour ½ cup water into pan. Cover turkey loosely with greased foil or brown paper. Roast in preheated oven for 2½ to 3 hours or until meat thermometer registers 180°F (82°C). Cover with foil; let stand for 20 minutes before carving and removing stuffing. Reserve ½ cup pan drippings for gravy.

Cranberry Gravy: Heat reserved pan drippings in same pan over medium heat until bubbling. Add flour and cook for about 1 minute or until thickened. Stir in brandy. Gradually stir in broth and cranberry sauce, whisking to remove any lumps. Boil gently, stirring occasionally, about 10 minutes or until thickened. Add salt and pepper to taste. Strain to remove any lumps.

Pine Nut and Apricot Stuffing: Cook bacon in small frying pan over medium heat until golden; drain on paper towel. Discard all but 2 tsp of fat. Cook onion and celery in reserved fat in same pan over medium heat for about 5 minutes or until softened; scrape into large bowl. Add bacon and remaining ingredients. Mix well.

Glazed Ham

You might have to order your ham from a butcher or specialty food store. If cooking a smaller ham without the rind, halve the glaze recipe, brush over ham and proceed with cooking and basting as instructed. Choose from one of our two glazes.

20 lb (8.6 kg) leg of cooked ham with rind

whole cloves

Apricot Glaze

1 cup pineapple juice

1/2 cup apricot jam

2 Tbsp grainy mustard

Maple Orange Glaze

3/4 cup maple syrup

1/3 cup orange juice

1/3 cup marmalade

1 Tbsp Worcestershire sauce

Cut through rind at shank end of leg. Run fingers under rind to loosen. Carefully pull away rind, using fingers. Discard rind.

Make shallow cuts, about 1 inch (2.5 cm) apart, in one direction diagonally across fat. Make sure cuts aren't too deep or you will lose the decorative pattern. Then make shallow cuts in opposite direction to form diamond pattern.

Do-ahead tips: *The ham can be cooked a day or two ahead and served cold. Or, prepare the ham a day or two ahead by scoring it and inserting cloves. Place in baking dish, cover and refrigerate. Remove from refrigerator 1 hour before cooking. Remove the cover before cooking. Glaze can be made a day ahead and stored at room temperature in a sealed container.*

Grease wire rack and place in roasting pan. Preheat oven to 350°F (180°C).

Place one clove where each cut meets at the tip of each diamond shape. Place ham in prepared pan. Wrap a piece of greased foil around bone-end. Brush ham with some of glaze. Bake, uncovered, in preheated oven, for about 1 hour, brushing frequently with glaze, until browned and glazed. Carve into thin slices. Serve hot or cold.

Apricot Glaze: Stir all ingredients in small saucepan over medium heat until jam is melted.

Maple Orange Glaze: Stir all ingredients in small saucepan over medium heat until marmalade is melted.

Seafood Pot Pies

These delicious pies are elegant as well as warming and homey. We used cod in this recipe, but you can use fish such as halibut, monk fish or snapper if you prefer.

½ x 17 oz (540 g) package flaky pie crust mix

5 Tbsp water

1 egg yolk

2 Tbsp butter

1 leek, thinly sliced

¾ cup finely chopped carrot

¼ cup all purpose flour

⅓ cup dry white wine (or milk)

1⅔ cups milk

11 oz (340 g) medium raw shrimp, peeled and halved

¾ lb (375 g) cod, cut into ¾ inch (2 cm) pieces

8 oz (250 g) small scallops (or quartered large scallops)

¼ tsp salt

¼ tsp coarsely ground pepper

½ cup frozen peas

Combine pastry mix and water in medium bowl and mix until a soft dough forms. Place on lightly floured surface and press dough together. Roll out to ¼ inch (6 mm) thickness. Cut four, 4½ inch (11 cm) rounds from pastry. Cover and set aside.

Melt butter in large saucepan over medium heat. Add leek and carrot and cook for about 5 minutes or until leek is softened. Stir in flour and cook for 1 minute until grainy.

Stir in wine, then gradually add milk. Stir for about 10 minutes or until mixture boils and thickens.

Do-ahead tips: *Pastry can be made, rolled out and cut a day ahead. Store well covered in refrigerator.*

Add shrimp and cod and stir. Cook, covered, for about 5 minutes until seafood is almost cooked. Add scallops and peas and stir. Cook, covered, for about 3 minutes or until scallops are just cooked; do not overcook. Remove from heat.

Preheat oven to 375°F (190°C).

Spoon about 1½ cups seafood mixture into four, 1¾ to 2 cup capacity ramekins. Place a round of pastry over each ramekin and press around edge to seal.

Brush pastry with egg yolk. Place ramekins on baking sheet to catch any filling that could spill out during baking. Bake in preheated oven for about 35 minutes or until pastry is golden brown and crisp.

Vegetarian Lasagna

You can use 1 cup of bottled pesto such as sun dried tomato or basil in place of the Parsley Pesto if you prefer.

3 medium eggplants, cut lengthwise into ¼ inch (6 mm) thick slices

¼ cup olive oil, plus 1 Tbsp

3 large red peppers, quartered, seeds and membranes removed

2 cups sliced mushrooms

1 cup grated mozzarella cheese

½ cup finely grated fresh Parmesan cheese

22 fl oz (700 g) jar pasta sauce

20 instant lasagna sheets

Parsley Pesto

1 cup packed fresh parsley sprigs

⅓ cup (1½ oz/50 g) pine nuts, toasted (see p. 7)

¼ cup finely grated fresh Parmesan cheese

3 Tbsp olive oil

2 Tbsp water

¼ tsp salt

White Sauce

3 Tbsp butter

¼ cup all purpose flour

2 cups milk

⅓ cup finely grated fresh Parmesan cheese

¼ tsp ground nutmeg

salt and pepper to taste

Lightly brush both sides of eggplant slices with ¼ cup of olive oil. Grease and preheat barbecue or grill pan to medium-high. Cook eggplant on preheated grill for about 3 minutes each side until tender and grill marks appear. Set aside.

Cook peppers, skin side down, on the same grill until skin is blackened and blistered. Place in medium bowl and cover. Let stand for 10 minutes. Peel and cut into thin strips.

Heat extra oil in large frying pan over high to medium-high heat. Add mushrooms and cook for about 5 minutes or until lightly browned and softened.

Combine both cheeses in small bowl.

Grease a 9 x 13 inch baking dish. Preheat oven to 350°F (180°C).

Spoon 1 cup of pasta sauce over bottom of prepared dish. Arrange one-third of lasagna sheets over sauce, breaking sheets where necessary to enable them to fit properly in dish. Scatter mushrooms over lasagna sheets. Spread with another 1 cup of pasta sauce. Layer half eggplant over sauce. Spread with half Parsley Pesto. Sprinkle with half cheese mixture. Top with another third of lasagna sheets. Spread with remaining pasta sauce.

Do-ahead tips: *Can be made 1 month ahead, well covered and frozen in freezer. Let thaw before reheating, covered, in 350°F (180°C) oven for 30 to 40 minutes until hot.*

Then layer red peppers, remaining cheese mixture, remaining eggplants then remaining pesto. Top with remaining lasagna sheets, breaking sheets to enable them to fit properly. Spread with White Sauce; cover with foil. Bake in preheated oven for 30 minutes. Remove cover and bake for 45 to 55 minutes or until browned around edges and lasagna sheets are tender when tested with skewer. Place under hot broiler for 3 to 5 minutes or until golden brown. Cover and let stand for 15 minutes before cutting.

Parsley Pesto: Place all ingredients in food processor and process until smooth.

White Sauce: Melt butter in medium saucepan over medium heat. Add flour and cook for 1 minute until grainy. Gradually stir in milk. Stir for about 5 minutes or until mixture boils and thickens. Add cheese, nutmeg, salt and pepper and stir until well combined.

Maple Glazed Salmon

When you purchase the salmon, ask the store to remove the skin if you would prefer not to do it yourself at home. This recipe was tested on a long cast iron grill pan. If you don't have one, you can either pan fry the salmon or broil it (broiling method included below).

1 cup maple syrup

1 cup olive oil

$^1/_2$ cup soy sauce

1 cup chopped fresh parsley

$^1/_2$ cup rye

3 lb (1.5 kg) side of salmon, skin removed

Combine syrup, oil and soy sauce in medium saucepan over medium-high heat. Bring to a boil and let boil for 3 minutes. Remove from heat and stir in parsley and rye. Let stand until cool.

Cut salmon into 6 to 8 pieces. Place in large shallow baking dish. Pour marinade over and cover. Refrigerate for 12 to 24 hours, stirring occasionally.

Heat a long grill pan over medium heat using 2 burners or elements. Lightly brush pan with a little oil. Remove salmon from marinade; discard marinade. Place salmon on grill pan. Cook for 5 to 8 minutes per side depending on thickness of salmon, until salmon is just cooked; do not overcook.

Or, place large piece of foil on baking sheet; grease foil. Place salmon on foil. Cook salmon under medium-hot broiler about 6 inches away from heat for 5 to 8 minutes per side depending on thickness of salmon, until salmon is just cooked; do not overcook.

Do-ahead tips: *Salmon can be marinated 2 days ahead and stored covered in refrigerator.*

Bacon and Rosemary Roasted Pork

Make sure you have some butcher's twine on hand to tie around the pork.

6 lb (2.7 kg) pork loin roast

4 garlic cloves, peeled and quartered

3 Tbsp Dijon mustard

¼ tsp salt

¼ tsp coarsely ground pepper

8 large sprigs fresh rosemary

8 to 10 slices bacon

Apple Mustard Gravy

⅓ cup all purpose flour

3 cups chicken broth

1½ cups apple juice

1 Tbsp Dijon mustard

salt and pepper to taste

Lightly grease a wire rack and place inside roasting pan. Preheat oven to 350°F (180°C).

Make 16 slits evenly all over pork and insert a piece of garlic into each slit.

Spread mustard evenly over pork. Sprinkle with salt and pepper. Lay rosemary sprigs lengthwise on top of pork. Wrap bacon around pork.

Secure pork with butcher's twine tied at 1 inch (2.5 cm) intervals. Place in prepared pan. Roast, uncovered, in preheated oven for 2½ to 3 hours or until meat thermometer inserted into center of roast reads 150°F (65°C). Do not overcook.

Cover with foil. Reserve pan drippings. Let pork stand for 20 minutes before carving into ½ inch (1.2 cm) thick slices. Serve with Apple Mustard Gravy.

Apple Mustard Gravy: Heat reserved drippings in same pan over medium heat. Add flour and cook for about 1 minute or until thickened. Gradually stir in broth and juice, whisking to remove any lumps. Stir in mustard. Boil gently, stirring occasionally, for about 5 to 10 minutes or until thickened. Strain and add salt and pepper to taste.

Do-ahead tips: *Pork can be prepared a day ahead and stored well wrapped in refrigerator. Let stand at room temperature for 1 hour before roasting.*

Cornish Hens with Pear Stuffing

These roasted hens would be delicious served with the Cranberry Gravy (page 40). If making the gravy, reserve the same amount of pan juices from the hens as you would with the turkey.

Cornish Hens

- 6 Cornish hens
- salt and pepper
- 12 bacon slices

Pear Stuffing

- 1 Tbsp canola oil
- 1 cup finely chopped onion
- 1½ cups finely chopped fresh peeled pear
- 2 cups fresh fine breadcrumbs (see p. 6)
- 1 cup (3½ oz/100 g) walnuts, toasted (see p. 7), chopped
- 2 Tbsp chopped fresh sage
- 2 tsp balsamic vinegar
- 2 tsp packed brown sugar
- ¼ tsp salt
- ½ tsp coarsely ground pepper

Cornish Hens: Preheat oven to 350°F (180°C). Grease a wire rack and place inside roasting pan.

Rinse hens inside and out under cold water and pat dry inside and out with paper towel. Fill each hen with about ½ cup Pear Stuffing. Secure opening with skewers and tie legs together with butcher's twine.

Sprinkle hens with salt and pepper. Wrap 2 slices of bacon around each hen.

Place in prepared pan. Roast, uncovered, in preheated oven for 1 to 1¼ hours or until meat thermometer registers 180°F (82°C) when inserted into the thickest part of the hen. Cover with foil and let stand for 10 minutes. If hens are larger and you are serving half per person (see sidebar), cut through breast and backbone to halve.

Do-ahead tips: *The stuffing can be made 1 month ahead and stored in a sealed bag or container in the freezer. Thaw stuffing thoroughly before placing it into hens. Stuff the hens just before cooking. Note that the stuffing does compact when frozen and thawed.*

Cornish hens can vary in size—if the hens are large, you might want to halve each hen and serve half per person, in which case you also might want to increase the stuffing amount. Sometimes the hens can be missing limbs, so feel through the package as best you can before purchasing them to check if they are intact.

Pear Stuffing: Heat oil in large frying pan over medium heat. Add onion and pear and cook for about 5 minutes or until softened. Remove from heat. Add remaining ingredients and mix until well combined.

Lamb and Red Wine Braise

Whether you're entertaining over the festive season or feeding a hungry family, this recipe is certain to chase away those winter chills. You can use stewing beef in place of lamb if preferred.

¼ cup all purpose flour

4 lbs (1.8 kg) lamb stewing meat, such as leg or shoulder, cut into ¾ inch (2 cm) pieces

2 Tbsp olive oil, plus another 1 Tbsp

1½ cups coarsely chopped onion

1½ cups coarsely chopped carrot

2 cups sliced mushrooms

4 cloves garlic, minced

1½ cups red wine

1 cup chicken broth

¼ cup tomato paste

4 small sprigs fresh rosemary

½ tsp salt

½ tsp coarsely ground pepper

Toss flour and lamb in batches in large plastic bag until lamb is coated. Heat 2 tablespoons of oil in large pot or Dutch oven over medium-high heat. Add lamb in 3 to 4 batches and sear until browned all over; remove from pan. Add a little more oil if necessary for browning. Remove from pan.

Heat extra oil in same pot over medium heat. Add onion and carrot and cook for about 5 minutes until onion is softened. Add mushrooms and garlic and cook for about 5 minutes or until mushrooms soften.

Stir in lamb and remaining ingredients. Bring to boil, then reduce heat to low. Cook, covered, stirring occasionally, for 1 hour. Remove cover and cook for 30 to 45 minutes, stirring occasionally, or until lamb is tender and sauce is thickened.

Do-ahead tips: *Lamb can be made a day ahead and stored in a sealed container in refrigerator. Reheat slowly in large pot over low heat until hot. Mixture can also be frozen in a sealed container for up to 1 month. Thaw in refrigerator before reheating.*

We thought these tasty miniature pies were delicious served with spicy ketchup.

1 Tbsp canola oil
1 cup finely chopped onion
4 cloves garlic, minced
1 tsp ground allspice
¾ lb (375 g) ground pork
¾ lb (375 g) ground beef
½ tsp salt
1 tsp coarsely ground pepper
½ cup beef or chicken broth
⅔ cup fine dry breadcrumbs, toasted (see p. 6)
17 oz (540 g) package flaky pie crust mix
10 Tbsp water
1 egg, lightly beaten
1 Tbsp milk

Grease a 12-hole muffin pan.

Heat oil in a large frying pan over medium heat. Add onion and cook for about 5 minutes or until softened. Add garlic and allspice and cook for about 1 minute or until fragrant.

Stir in ground pork, beef, salt and pepper. Cook, breaking up pieces of ground meat, until browned.

Add broth and stir. Cook, uncovered, for 5 to 10 minutes or until almost all broth is evaporated. Remove from heat and stir in breadcrumbs; cool.

Preheat oven to 400°F (200°C).

Combine both envelopes of pastry mix and water in a large bowl and stir until soft dough forms. Press dough together. Roll out two-thirds of dough on lightly floured surface until ⅛ inch (3 mm) thickness. Cut 12, 4½ inch (11 cm) circles from pastry. You will have to re-roll pastry off-cuts in order to get 12 circles. Press into prepared muffin pan, leaving a slight overhang of pastry at top.

Press ⅓ cup ground meat mixture into each pastry case.

Roll remaining pastry onto lightly floured surface until pastry is ⅛ inch (3 mm) thick. Cut twelve, 3½ inch (9 cm) circles from pastry. Place over ground meat mixture. Press edges of pastry together to seal and tuck edges under or in. Lightly press around edges using a lightly floured fork to seal.

Do-ahead tips: *These can be prepared 1 month ahead and frozen in sealed containers in freezer. Thaw in refrigerator before baking.*

Whisk egg and milk together in small bowl. Brush over pastry tops. Cut 3 slits into each pastry top. Bake on bottom shelf in preheated oven for about 35 minutes or until pastry is golden and crisp. Let stand in pan 5 minutes before serving.

Roast Beef with Horseradish and Bacon Stuffing

You can substitute broth or red wine for the port, although you won't achieve the same flavor. If a larger roast is not available in the meat section, ask the butcher to cut one for you.

Roast Beef

6 lb (2.8 kg) beef sirloin roast

salt and pepper to sprinkle

¼ cup all purpose flour

4 cups beef broth

1 cup port

¼ cup horseradish cream

⅔ cup whipping cream

¼ tsp salt

Horseradish and Bacon Stuffing

4 slices bacon, chopped

1 Tbsp canola oil

1 cup finely chopped onion

2 cups fine fresh breadcrumbs (see p. 6)

2 Tbsp horseradish cream

3 Tbsp chopped fresh parsley

1 egg, lightly beaten

Do-ahead tips: *Stuffing can be prepared a day ahead and stored in a sealed container in refrigerator. Stuffing can also be frozen up to one month ahead and stored in a sealed freezer bag in freezer. Note that the stuffing does compact when frozen and thawed. Let thaw completely before stuffing beef.*

Roast Beef: Grease a wire rack and place inside roasting pan. Preheat oven to 350°F (180°C).

Cut roast in half horizontally almost through to the other side, but do not cut completely through. Open roast up butterfly fashion.

Spread one side of roast with Horseradish and Bacon Stuffing. Fold other side over to enclose stuffing. Using butcher's string, tie roast at 1 inch (2.5 cm) intervals. Place in prepared pan. Pour 1 cup water into pan. Roast, uncovered, in preheated oven for 1 hour, then turn over. Roast, uncovered, a further 1½ hours or until meat thermometer registers 155°F (68°C) for medium when inserted into center section of roast, avoiding stuffing. Or, cook roast to desired doneness.

Let stand, covered, for 20 minutes before cutting into ⅓ inch (1 cm) thick slices. Reserve ½ cup pan drippings.

Heat reserved pan drippings in same pan over medium heat. Add flour and cook for about 1 minute or until thickened. Gradually stir in broth, whisking to remove any lumps. Stir in port and horseradish. Boil gently, stirring occasionally, for about 10 minutes or until thickened.

Add remaining ingredients and stir until hot. Strain to remove any lumps.

Horseradish and Bacon Stuffing: Cook bacon in medium frying pan over medium heat for about 5 minutes or until golden brown. Drain on paper towel, chop finely and place in large bowl. Discard bacon fat from pan.

Heat oil in same pan over medium heat. Add onion and cook for about 5 minutes or until softened. Add to bacon. Add remaining ingredients and stir until well combined.

Roast Goose with Blackberry Port Sauce

You can buy geese at grocery stores or specialty food stores. They are most commonly sold frozen. The stuffing for Cornish Hens (page 52) would make a delicious stuffing for the goose.

Roast Goose

| 8 lb (3.6 kg) goose |
| salt and pepper |

Blackberry Port Sauce

3 Tbsp all purpose flour
1 cup port
2 cups chicken broth
5 Tbsp blackberry jam
$1/4$ tsp salt
$1/4$ to $1/2$ tsp coarsely ground pepper

Roast Goose: Grease wire rack and place in roasting pan. Remove and discard neck, giblets and any fat from goose cavities. Rinse inside and out with cold water. Pat dry with paper towels.

Half fill a large pot, Dutch oven or steamer with water and bring to a boil. Wearing clean rubber gloves to protect your hands, place goose, neck cavity side down, into boiling water; hold for 1 minute. Carefully turn goose and place other end into boiling water; hold for 1 minute. Remove from water. Place in prepared pan; pat dry with paper towel. Let stand, uncovered, for 15 minutes or until completely dry.

Do-ahead tips: *Goose can be prepared a day ahead and stored uncovered in refrigerator. Leaving the goose uncovered helps to dry the goose, promoting a crisper skin when roasted. Let stand at room temperature for 1 hour before roasting.*

Sprinkle goose with salt and pepper. Place breast-side down in prepared pan. Bake in preheated oven for 1¼ hours. Turn goose and cook for a further 1¼ hours or until skin is browned and meat thermometer registers 170°F (77°C). If you are roasting a stuffed goose, the internal temperature must be 180°F (82°C). Cover with foil. Let stand for 20 minutes before carving.

Pour pan drippings into 2 cup measure. Let stand for 15 minutes. Pour or spoon off fat and reserve 3 tablespoons of drippings.

Blackberry Port Sauce: Heat reserved pan drippings in same pan over medium-high heat. Add flour and cook for 1 minute. Gradually stir in port, whisking to remove any lumps. Add remaining ingredients and stir until well combined. Boil gently, stirring occasionally, for about 10 minutes or until thickened. Strain to remove any lumps.

Easy Chicken Cassoulet

Traditionally a cassoulet (a dish of beans and poultry and/or meat) takes almost 3 days to make and contains duck or goose that has been cooked in fat. This version takes a fraction of the time, uses chicken and canned beans and is considerably lower in fat.

1 Tbsp olive oil, plus another 1 Tbsp

12 skinless bone-in chicken thighs

4 Italian sausages

6 slices bacon

2 cups chopped onion

4 cloves garlic, minced

2 cups chicken broth

¼ cup tomato paste

1 Tbsp chopped fresh thyme

2 x 19 fl oz (540 ml) cans white beans, rinsed, drained

1 cup dry white wine

salt and pepper to taste

1½ cups fine fresh breadcrumbs (see p. 6)

Heat oil in a large pot or Dutch oven over medium-high heat. Add chicken in 2 batches and sear for about 10 minutes or until browned all over; remove from pot.

Cook sausages in same pot for about 10 minutes or until brown all over. Remove from pot and cut into 1 inch (2.5 cm) pieces.

Cook bacon in same pot over medium heat until golden. Remove from pan and chop. Drain fat from pan.

Heat extra oil in same pot over medium heat. Add onion and cook for about 10 minutes or until onion is softened. Add garlic and cook for about 2 minutes or until fragrant.

Add broth, paste, thyme, beans and wine and stir until well combined. Add chicken, sausage and bacon. Sprinkle with salt and pepper. Cover and bring to boil.

Preheat oven to 350°F (180°C).

Spoon mixture into prepared dish. Cook, covered, in preheated oven for about 1½ hours, until sauce is thickened and chicken is very tender.

Sprinkle with breadcrumbs and cook, uncovered, for 20 to 30 minutes or until crumbs are golden and crisp.

Do-ahead tips: *Have all ingredients prepared a day ahead and stored, covered, in refrigerator.*

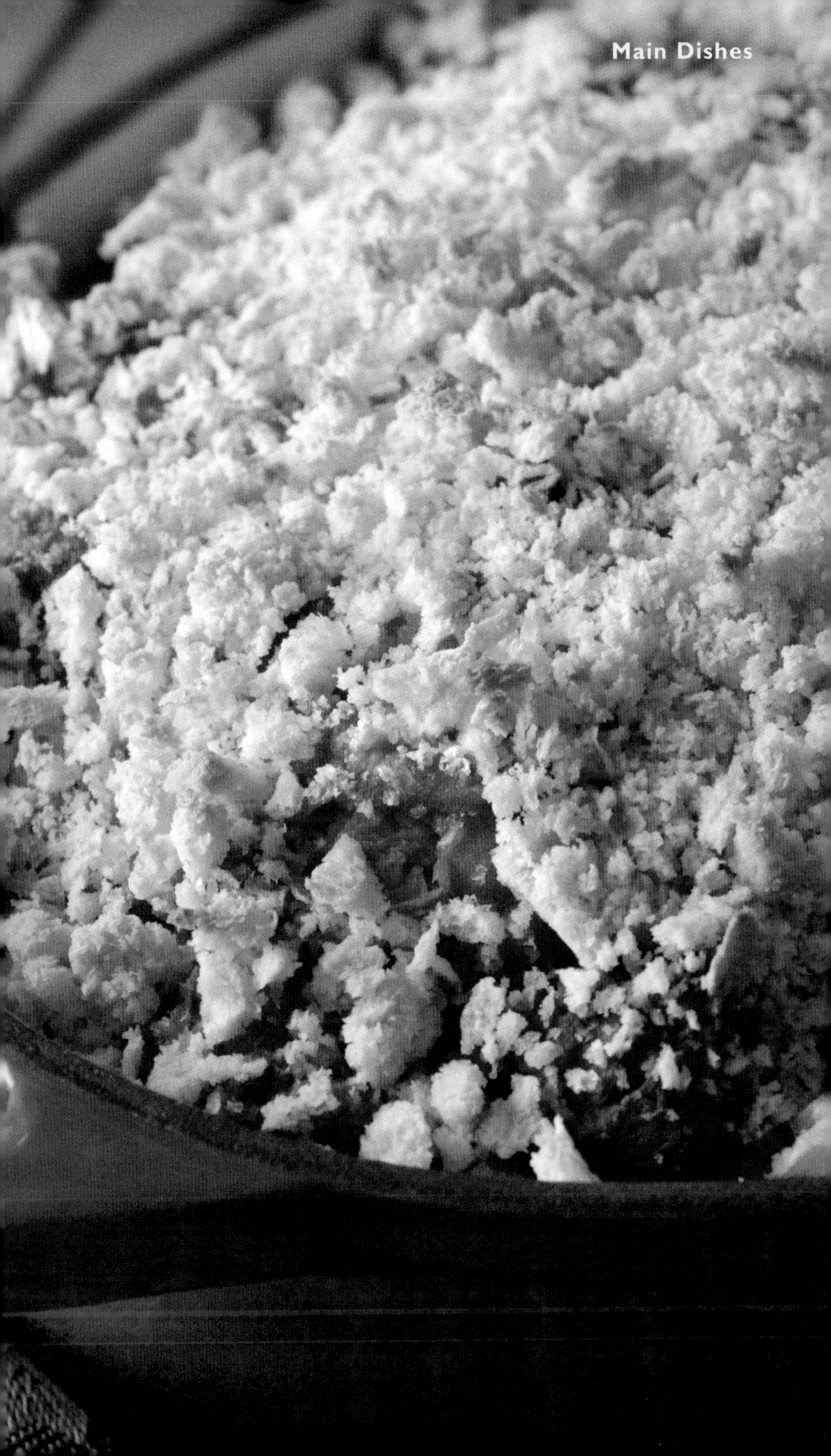

Sweet Roasted Yams

These delicious sweet yams can be drizzled with honey instead of maple syrup if preferred.

3 lbs yams (orange sweet potatoes), peeled, cut into 1 inch (2.5 cm) cubes

2 Tbsp olive oil

2 Tbsp coarsely chopped fresh rosemary

1/2 tsp salt

1/2 tsp coarsely ground pepper

1/4 tsp ground cinnamon

2 Tbsp maple syrup

Line a baking sheet with parchment paper. Preheat oven to 350°F (180°C).

Combine yams, oil, rosemary, salt, pepper and cinnamon in large bowl. Toss to coat yams completely with mixture. Arrange in single layer on prepared baking sheet. Bake for 40 minutes in preheated oven, stirring once during cooking.

Drizzle with syrup and toss gently to coat. Bake about 15 minutes or until glazed and lightly browned.

Spinach, Toffee Pecan and Goat Cheese Salad

Dried cranberries add a seasonal and delicious touch to this elegant salad.

- $^2/_3$ cup (2$^1/_2$ oz/70 g) pecans, toasted
- $^1/_3$ cup granulated sugar
- 2 Tbsp water
- 9 oz (225 g) bag baby spinach leaves
- 4 oz (125 g) goat cheese, coarsely crumbled
- $^1/_3$ cup (2 oz/60 g) dried cranberries

Maple Vinaigrette

- $^1/_4$ cup olive oil
- 2 Tbsp red wine vinegar
- 2 Tbsp maple syrup
- 1 tsp grainy mustard
- pinch of salt

Line a baking sheet with parchment paper. Preheat oven to 350°F (180°C).

Place pecans, touching each other, on prepared baking

Do-ahead tips: *The toffee pecans can be made a week ahead and stored in a sealed container. The Maple Vinaigrette can be made 3 days ahead and stored in the refrigerator.*

sheet. Toast in preheated oven for 10 minutes. Remove from oven. Set pan aside, leaving pecans on pan.

Meanwhile, stir sugar and water in small saucepan over medium heat until sugar is dissolved. Boil gently, without stirring, for about 5 minutes or until mixture is a deep golden color. Drizzle syrup mixture over pecans. Let stand for about 20 minutes or until cooled completely and brittle; coarsely chop.

Toss toffee pecans, spinach, cheese and cranberries in large serving bowl. Drizzle with Maple Vinaigrette and toss.

Maple Vinaigrette: Shake all ingredients in jar until well combined.

Brussels Sprouts with Bacon and Mustard

Small Brussels sprouts that have been cooked until just tender and bright are delicious, so it is important not to overcook them. Overcooking can lead to the strong, unpleasant taste that has given the poor sprouts their undeserved reputation.

4 slices bacon, chopped

¼ cup thinly sliced green onions

2 Tbsp grainy mustard

2 Tbsp orange juice

1 Tbsp butter

2 lbs small Brussels sprouts, stalk ends trimmed

Cook bacon in small frying pan over medium heat until golden; drain on paper towel.

Reserve 2 teaspoons of bacon fat in same frying pan; discard any remaining fat. Add onion and cook over medium heat for about 3 minutes or until softened.

Add mustard, orange juice and butter and stir until butter is melted.

Meanwhile, cook sprouts in steamer in large saucepan over simmering water for 10 to 12 minutes or until tender crisp and bright green; do not overcook. Drain water from pan and remove steamer. Return sprouts to same pan.

Add bacon mixture and toss to coat.

Mushroom Pilaf

A pilaf is easy to make—you simply add the ingredients to rice and cook until the liquid is absorbed and the rice is tender. Use any assortment of mushrooms you wish. Basmati rice gives the pilaf a distinct flavor. It is available in the same section as other rice in grocery stores.

2 Tbsp butter, plus another
  1 Tbsp

4 cups sliced mushrooms

1 cup finely chopped onion

1½ cups basmati rice

3 cups chicken or vegetable
  broth

3 Tbsp chopped fresh parsley

1½ Tbsp lemon juice

¼ tsp salt

¼ tsp coarsely ground pepper

Melt 2 tablespoons of butter in a large saucepan over medium-high heat. Add mushrooms and cook for about 5 minutes or until mushrooms are softened. Remove from pan and set aside.

Melt extra butter in same pan over medium heat. Add onion and cook for about 5 minutes or until onion is softened.

Add rice and stir until coated. Stir in broth.
Cover and bring to boil. Turn heat to low and
cook, covered, for about 15 minutes or until rice
is tender.

Stir in remaining ingredients.
Let stand, covered, for 5
minutes; fluff with fork.

Roasted Potato Salad

This is delicious served hot or cold and can be served with barbecued meat and chicken.

- 4 lbs (2 kg) small new potatoes, halved
- 2 Tbsp canola oil
- ½ tsp salt
- ¼ tsp coarsely ground pepper
- 4 cloves garlic, not peeled, bruised (see sidebar)
- ⅓ cup finely chopped green onions
- ¼ cup finely chopped gherkins
- ¼ cup mayonnaise
- ¼ cup sour cream
- 2 Tbsp chopped fresh dill
- 1 Tbsp creamed horseradish

Grease a baking sheet. Preheat oven to 400°F (200°C).

Toss potatoes, oil, salt, pepper and garlic on prepared baking sheet. Roast, uncovered, in preheated oven, turning occasionally, for about 1 hour or until golden brown. Remove garlic cloves.

Combine remaining ingredients in large bowl. Add hot potatoes and stir to coat. Serve hot or cold.

To bruise garlic, place on chopping board and press down on clove using the wide blade of a knife or meat mallet until clove is lightly squashed.

Do-ahead tips: *If you are serving the salad cold, it can be made a day ahead and stored in a sealed container in the refrigerator. If serving it hot, you can prepare the dressing a day ahead and store in a sealed container in refrigerator. Remove from refrigerator 1 hour before tossing it with the hot potatoes.*

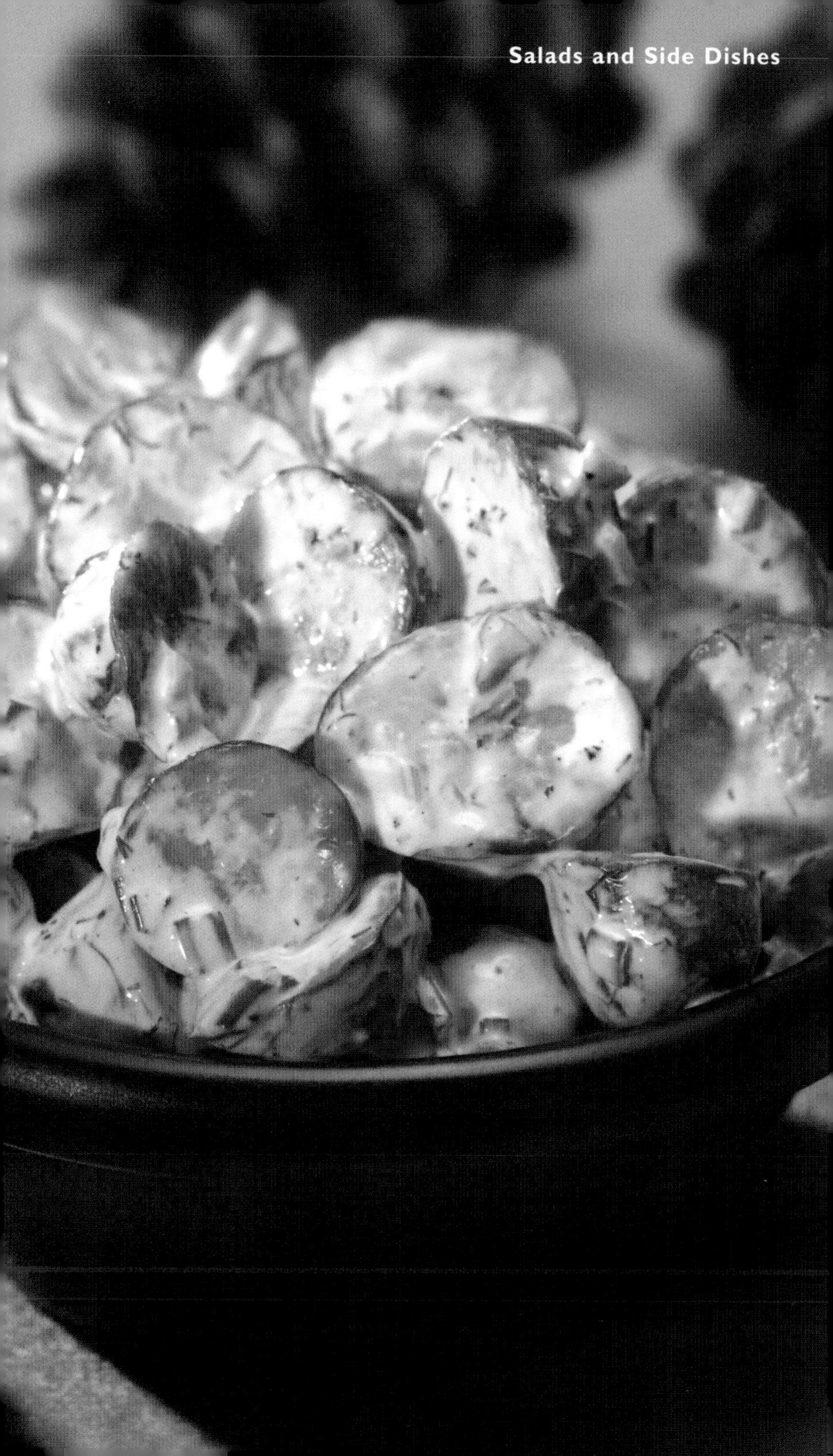

Corn Bake

This is so quick and easy to prepare. Everything is mixed in one bowl and spread into the prepared dish. It is also delicious served cold the next day on sandwiches or toast. Cornflake crumbs are available in packages in grocery stores. You can use fine dry breadcrumbs in place of cornflake crumbs if preferred.

2 x 12½ oz (398 ml) cans corn kernels, drained

2 x 12½ oz (398 ml) cans creamed corn

2 eggs

1 cup sour cream

⅔ cup cornflake crumbs

½ tsp salt

½ tsp coarsely ground pepper

Grease a 6 to 8 cup baking dish. Preheat oven to 350°F (180°C).

Combine all ingredients in a large bowl. Scrape into prepared baking dish; smooth top. Bake, uncovered, in preheated oven for about 50 minutes or until set and top is golden.

Do-ahead tips: *Can be prepared 1 to 3 hours ahead and stored, covered, in refrigerator. Remove from refrigerator 1 hour before baking.*

Green Beans with Sage Walnut Butter

If fresh beans are unavailable, use frozen whole beans.

- 3 Tbsp butter
- 1/3 cup (1 oz/30 g) walnuts, chopped
- 1 tsp chopped fresh sage
- 1 lb (500 g) green beans, stalk ends removed

Melt butter in small saucepan over medium-low heat. Add walnuts and sage and cook for about 5 minutes or until butter is starting to turn golden brown.

Meanwhile, cook beans in steamer in large saucepan over simmering water for 5 to 8 minutes or until bright green and tender. Drain water from pan and remove the steamer. Add beans to same pan. Add butter mixture and toss to coat.

Do-ahead tips: *Remove stalk ends from beans a day ahead. Store beans in a sealed bag in refrigerator.*

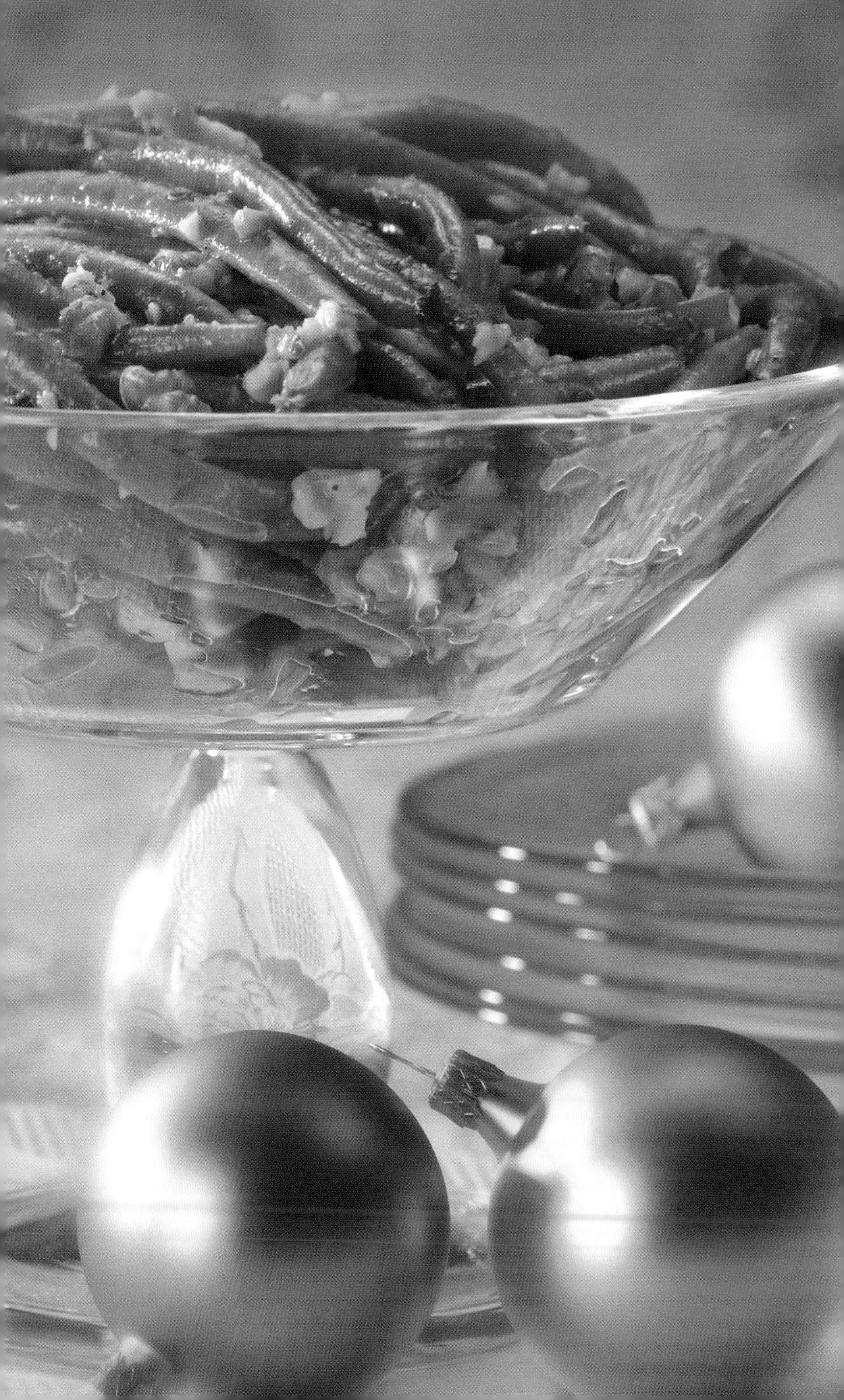

Smoked Cheese Mashed Potatoes

Enjoy a slight twist on regular mashed potatoes. Smoked cheese can be found in grocery and specialty food stores.

4 lbs (2 kg) russet potatoes, peeled and quartered
$\frac{1}{4}$ cup butter
$\frac{1}{4}$ cup milk
2 Tbsp sour cream
1$\frac{1}{2}$ cups grated smoked cheese
$\frac{1}{2}$ tsp salt
$\frac{1}{4}$ tsp coarsely ground pepper

Cook potatoes in salted water in large saucepan over medium-high heat for 20 to 25 minutes or until tender but not mushy. Drain well and return to the same pan. Mash until no large lumps remain.

Add butter, milk and sour cream and stir vigorously with fork until smooth.

Add remaining ingredients and stir until well combined.

We used applewood smoked cheese in this recipe.

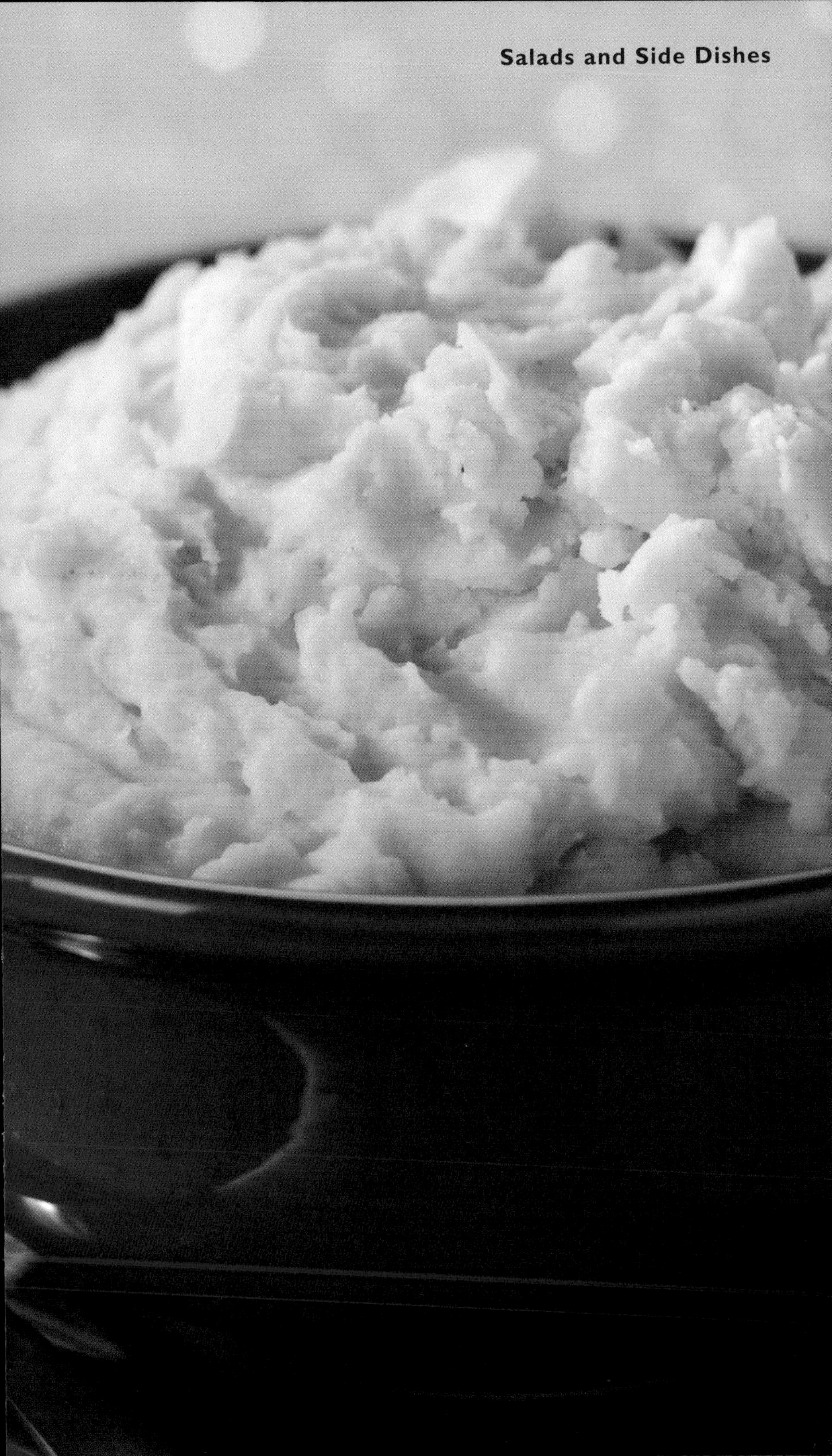

Roasted Caramelized Onions

Onions are added to most savory dishes, but they also make a delicious side dish. As they cook, they soften and sweeten. Any leftovers can be added to pasta dishes, stews or casseroles.

6 medium onions

1 Tbsp canola oil

1 Tbsp balsamic vinegar

1/4 tsp salt

1/4 tsp coarsely ground pepper

2 Tbsp packed brown sugar

Lightly grease baking sheet. Preheat oven to 350°F (180°C).

Peel and quarter onions but do not remove the stalk ends, as the ends help wedges hold together as they cook. Place in large bowl.

Add oil, vinegar, salt and pepper and toss to coat. Place on prepared baking sheet. Roast, uncovered, in preheated oven for 50 minutes.

Sprinkle with sugar and toss. Roast a further 10 to 15 minutes or until browned and glazed.

Orange Salad with Pine Nut Vinaigrette

The Valencia salad from Spain was the inspiration for this recipe. Choose heavy, juicy oranges such as navel or Valencia for best results.

Orange Salad

6 medium oranges

¼ cup thinly sliced green onions

¼ cup small pitted black olives

3 Tbsp shredded fresh mint leaves

Pine Nut Vinaigrette

3 Tbsp pine nuts, toasted (see p. 7), finely chopped

2 Tbsp olive oil

1 Tbsp red wine vinegar

1 Tbsp liquid honey

pinch of salt

Orange Salad: Cut ends from each orange. Place one orange, one cut end down, on cutting board. Using a small, sharp knife, cut down and around orange to remove rind and as much of the white pith as possible. Cut orange into 1 inch (2.5 cm) pieces and place in medium serving bowl.

Add remaining ingredients. Drizzle with Pine Nut Vinaigrette and gently toss.

Pine Nut Vinaigrette: Shake all ingredients together in small jar until well combined.

Do-ahead tips: *Oranges can be prepared a day ahead and stored in a sealed container in refrigerator. Dressing, excluding pine nuts, can be made 1 to 2 days ahead and stored in a jar in a cool place. Add pine nuts just before serving.*

Creamy Lemon Coleslaw

This salad is a refreshing change during the festive season, but it would make a nice accompaniment to a barbecue during the warmer months too.

Coleslaw

- 4 cups finely shredded red cabbage
- 4 cups finely shredded green cabbage
- 1½ cups (8 oz/250 g) dark raisins
- 1 cup (4 oz/125 g) sliced almonds, toasted (see p. 7)
- 1 cup thinly sliced celery
- 1 cup thinly sliced red onion

Creamy Lemon Dressing

- 1 cup mayonnaise
- ⅓ cup lemon juice
- 3 Tbsp granulated sugar
- 2 Tbsp Dijon mustard
- 1 Tbsp finely grated lemon rind
- ¼ tsp salt
- ⅛ tsp coarsely ground pepper

Coleslaw: Toss all ingredients in extra large serving bowl. Drizzle with dressing and toss.

Creamy Lemon Dressing: Whisk all ingredients together in small bowl.

Do-ahead tips: Prepare all ingredients a day ahead and store them separately in sealed bags in refrigerator. Dressing can be made 1 to 2 days ahead and stored in a sealed container in refrigerator. Toss everything together just before serving.

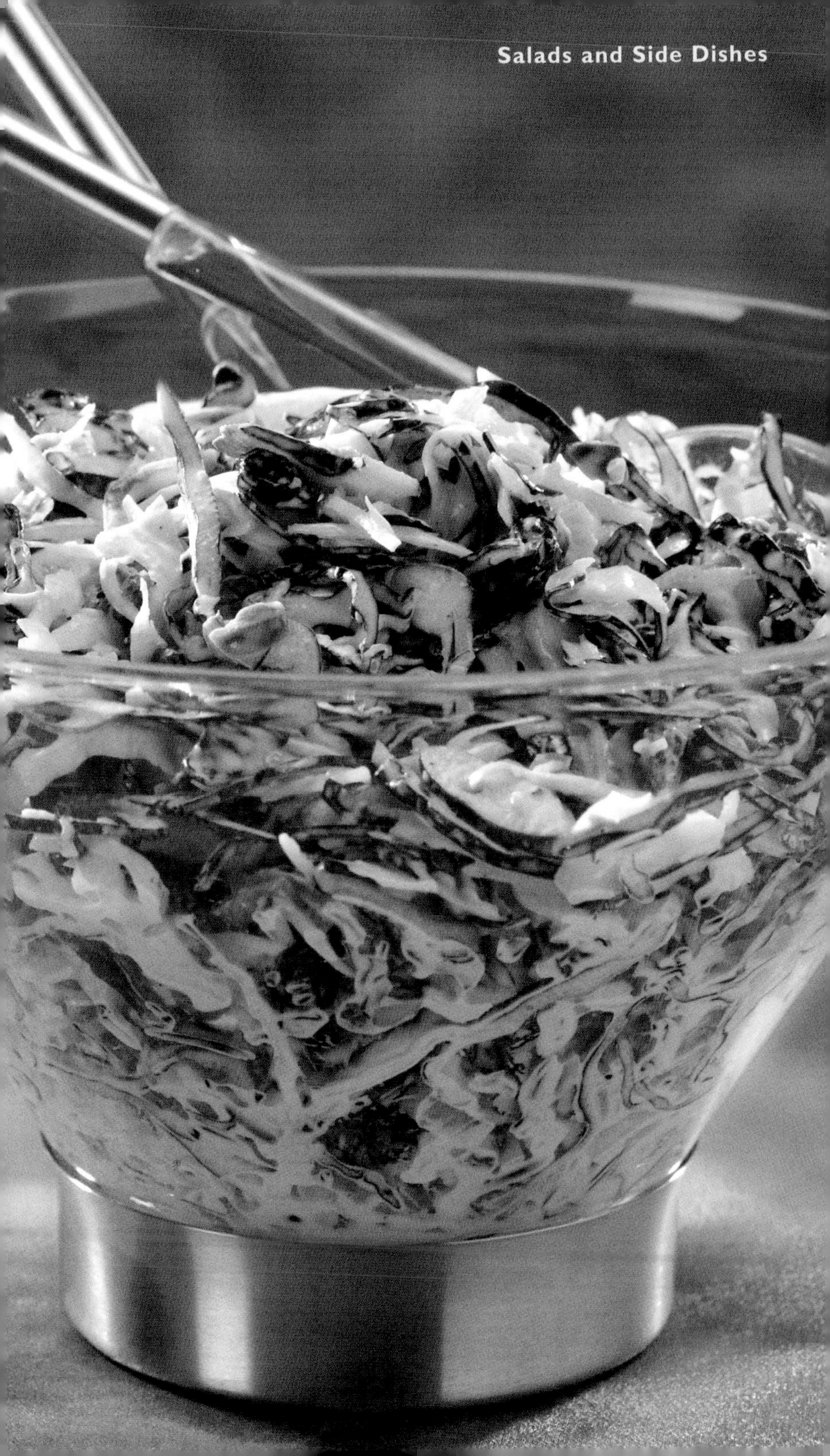

Orange Mashed Yams

1 Tbsp olive oil	Heat oil in large pot or Dutch oven over medium heat. Add onion and cook for about 5 minutes or until softened. Add cumin and pepper and cook for about 1 minute or until fragrant.
1 cup finely chopped onion	
1 tsp ground cumin	
1/2 tsp coarsely ground pepper	
4 lbs (2 kg) yams (orange sweet potatoes), peeled, cut into large pieces	Stir in yams, broth and salt. Cover and bring to boil over medium-high heat. Boil for about 15 minutes or until tender but not mushy. Drain well and return to same pan. Mash until no large lumps remain.
2 1/2 cups chicken or vegetable broth	
1/2 tsp salt	
1 cup finely grated fresh Parmesan cheese	Add remaining ingredients and stir vigorously with fork until well combined and smooth.
2–3 Tbsp sour cream	
1–2 tsp finely grated orange rind	

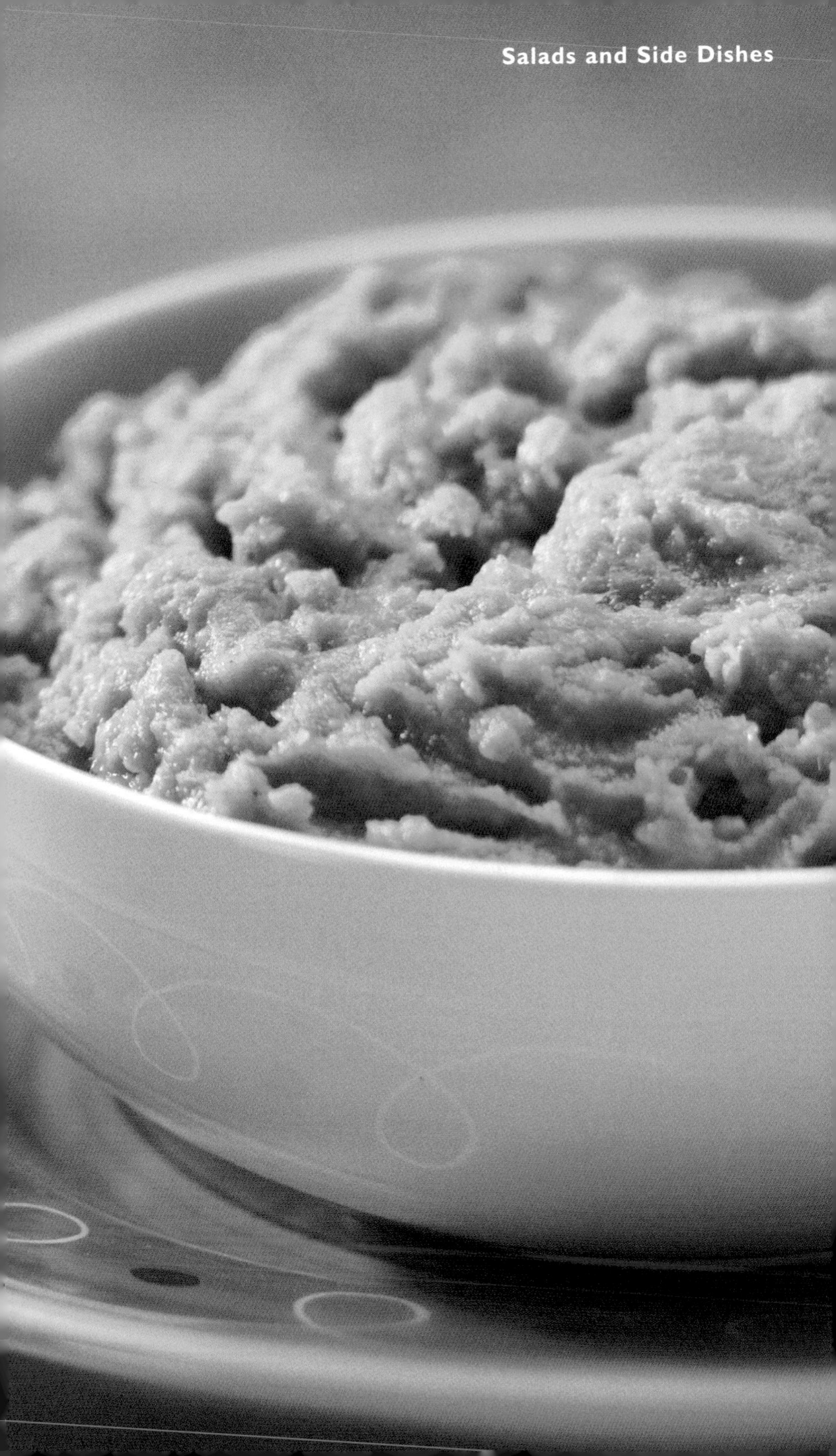

Scalloped Potatoes

This dish is best prepared just before baking. Don't slice the potatoes ahead of time and leave them to sit in water, because this will prevent potatoes from absorbing the broth and cream as they cook. A mandoline works very well for ensuring potatoes are sliced evenly.

4 lbs (2 kg) red potatoes, peeled, thinly sliced

10 slices bacon, coarsely chopped, cooked until golden

1½ cups grated white cheddar cheese

½ tsp salt

¼ tsp coarsely ground pepper

¼ to ½ tsp ground nutmeg

1½ cups whipping cream

1 cup chicken broth

Grease a shallow 8 cup baking dish. Preheat oven to 350°F (180°C).

Layer potatoes in prepared dish. Scatter bacon and cheese over potatoes. Sprinkle with salt, pepper and nutmeg.

Combine cream and broth in medium bowl and pour over potatoes. Bake, uncovered, in preheated oven for about 1 hour or until potatoes are tender and top is golden brown. Cover and let stand for 10 minutes before serving to allow liquid to settle.

Roasted Beet Salad with Maple Vinaigrette

The earthy flavor of the beets and the sweetness of the pears make a delicious combination. This salad would also be really good sprinkled with some chopped toasted walnuts.

Roasted Beet Salad

- 8 medium beets, trimmed of stalks, not peeled
- 2 ripe medium pears, peeled, thinly sliced
- 3 oz (90 g) goat cheese, coarsely crumbled

Maple Vinaigrette

- ¼ cup maple syrup
- 3 Tbsp white vinegar
- 2 Tbsp olive oil
- ½ tsp salt
- ¼ tsp coarsely ground pepper

Roasted Beet Salad: Preheat oven to 350°F (180°F). Wrap beets individually in foil. Place beets on baking sheet. Roast in preheated oven for about 1 hour, or until tender when pierced with skewer. Let stand for 10 to 15 minutes or until cool enough to handle.

Peel beets. (The skin should peel away easily by hand. You might want to wear clean rubber gloves to prevent your hands from being stained.) Cut beets into wedges.

Arrange beets, pears and goat cheese in a medium serving bowl. Drizzle with Maple Vinaigrette.

Maple Vinaigrette: Shake all ingredients together in jar until well combined.

Do-ahead tips: *The beets can be roasted and peeled a day or two before serving and stored in a sealed container in the refrigerator. The Maple Vinaigrette can be prepared a day or two before serving and stored in a sealed jar in refrigerator. Arrange salad just before serving.*

Grapefruit, Fennel and Hazelnut Salad

This fresh, lively salad features a mix of flavors sure to delight your guests.

4 cups loosely packed mixed baby lettuce leaves

1 medium fennel bulb, thinly sliced

2 red grapefruit, segmented (see p. 98)

3 oz (90 g) blue cheese, coarsely crumbled or chopped

½ cup (2½ oz/75 g) filberts (hazelnuts), toasted (see p. 7), coarsely chopped

Balsamic Vinaigrette

¼ cup olive oil

2 Tbsp lemon juice

1½ Tbsp balsamic vinegar

1 Tbsp liquid honey

¼ tsp salt

¼ tsp coarsely ground pepper

Gently toss all ingredients in large serving bowl. Drizzle with Balsamic Vinaigrette.

Balsamic Vinaigrette: Shake all ingredients together in jar until well combined.

Do-ahead tips: *Vinaigrette can be made a day ahead and stored in a jar in the refrigerator. Remaining salad ingredients can be prepared a day ahead and each ingredient stored in sealed plastic bags in the refrigerator.*

Cauliflower Broccoli Bake with Garlic Crumbs

1½ lbs (750 g) cauliflower florets

1 lb (500 g) broccoli florets

Cheese Sauce

2 Tbsp butter

2 Tbsp all purpose flour

2 cups milk

1 cup grated white cheddar cheese

1 tsp prepared mustard

¼ tsp coarsely ground pepper

¼ tsp ground nutmeg

Garlic Crumbs

1½ Tbsp butter

3 cloves garlic, minced

1 cup fine fresh breadcrumbs (see p. 6)

Grease a 6 to 8 cup baking dish. Cook cauliflower and broccoli in steamer in large saucepan over simmering water until bright and tender. Place in prepared dish. Pour cheese sauce over cauliflower and broccoli. Sprinkle breadcrumbs over cheese sauce. Bake in preheated oven for about 20 minutes or until bubbling and hot.

Cheese Sauce: Melt butter in medium saucepan over medium heat. Add flour and stir until mixture is bubbling.

Gradually stir in milk and continue to stir until mixture is smooth. Simmer, stirring constantly, for about 5 minutes or until thickened and boiling. Remove from heat.

Add remaining ingredients and stir until well combined.

Do-ahead tips: *Cheese Sauce can be made a day ahead and stored in a sealed container in refrigerator. Let stand at room temperature for 30 minutes before using.*

Garlic Crumbs: Preheat oven to 350°F (180°C). Melt butter in medium frying pan over medium heat. Add garlic and cook for 1 to 2 minutes or until garlic is softened and fragrant. Stir in breadcrumbs and cook for about 5 minutes or until golden brown.

Cranberry Brie Muffins

These muffins can also be made in mini muffin pans and served as an appetizer with a cheese and fruit platter. If using mini muffin pans, decrease cooking time by about 10 minutes.

2⅓ cups all purpose flour

4 tsp baking powder

¼ tsp salt

3 Tbsp packed brown sugar

½ cup (3 oz/90 g) dried cranberries

5 oz (155 g) Brie cheese, chopped

1 egg

1 cup milk

⅓ cup canola oil

⅓ cup cranberry jelly

Line 12-hole muffin pan with muffin liners and spray with cooking spray. Preheat oven to 375°F (190°C).

Sift flour, baking powder, salt and sugar into large bowl.

Add cranberries and cheese and stir.

Whisk remaining ingredients in medium bowl and add to flour mixture. Stir until just combined; do not overmix. Spoon mixture into prepared muffin pan, filling each hole to three-quarters full. Bake in preheated oven for 20 to 25 minutes or until cooked when tested with skewer. Best served warm.

Do-ahead tips: *These can be made 1 day ahead and warmed for 20 seconds each in the microwave but are best served fresh from the oven.*

Vanilla Citrus Salad

Vanilla beans are available from grocery and specialty food stores. The visible black specks in the salad are the tiny seeds from the pod.

½ cup granulated sugar

¼ cup water

1 vanilla bean, split lengthwise

6 oranges, segmented (see instructions at right)

6 red grapefruit, segmented

¼ cup orange-flavored liqueur (e.g., Cointreau)

Stir sugar and water in small saucepan over medium heat until sugar is dissolved. Boil gently, without stirring, for 2 minutes. Remove from heat. Scrape seeds from vanilla bean into pan, add pod; cool. Pour into large bowl.

Add remaining ingredients, stir and cover. Refrigerate for 6 hours or overnight. Remove vanilla bean just before serving.

Segmenting oranges and grapefruit: Cut both ends from each orange and grapefruit. Place one cut end down on cutting board, and using a small sharp knife, cut down and around fruit, removing rind and as much of the white pith as possible. Place fruit on its side and cut down between membranes of each segment.

Do-ahead tips: *The salad is best when made a day ahead of serving for flavors to develop. It can be made 2 days ahead and stored in a sealed container in refrigerator.*

Salmon and Asparagus Crepes

This is a welcome addition to any brunch menu. Serve with the Cranberry Brie Muffins on page 96.

Crepes

1½ cups all purpose flour

1¾ cups milk

2 eggs

¼ tsp salt

Filling

2 Tbsp butter

¾ cup finely chopped onion

3 Tbsp all purpose flour

1¾ cups milk

4 oz (125 g) smoked salmon, coarsely chopped

1 Tbsp lemon juice

salt and pepper to taste

1 cup grated Swiss cheese

½ cup finely grated fresh Parmesan cheese

2 Tbsp sour cream

1 lb (500 g) asparagus, trimmed, halved lengthwise if thick

Crepes: Whisk all ingredients in medium bowl until smooth. Heat 8 inch (20 cm) non-stick frying pan on medium-high and grease with butter or spray with cooking spray. Add ⅓ cup batter to pan, swirling pan to ensure batter spreads evenly. Cook for about 1 minute or until golden underneath; flip. Cook for about 1 minute or until golden on bottom. Stack crepes on plate as you cook them and cover with foil to keep warm.

Filling: Melt butter in medium saucepan over medium heat. Add onion and cook for about 5 minutes or until softened. Add flour and cook for about 1 minute.

Gradually stir in milk and cook, stirring constantly, for about 5 minutes or until sauce is thickened and boiling; remove from heat.

Stir in salmon, lemon juice, salt, pepper and cheese. Cover and keep warm.

Meanwhile, cook asparagus in steamer in large saucepan over simmering water for about 2 minutes until bright green and crisp; do not overcook.

Lay crepe on cutting board. Spoon about ½ cup salmon filling down center of crepe. Lay 3 to 5 asparagus on filling. Roll up crepe to enclose filling. Repeat with remaining crepes, filling and asparagus.

Do-ahead tips: *Crepes can be made 2 days ahead and stored on a plate, wrapped in plastic wrap in refrigerator. Heat on low power for 30 to 60 seconds in microwave until warm.*

Strawberry Bread Pudding

You can use any of your favorite flavored jams for this recipe.

½ cup (3 oz/90 g) dark raisins

7 slices French bread, cut ⅓ inch (1 cm) thick

3 Tbsp butter, softened

⅓ cup strawberry jam

4 eggs

3 cups milk

½ cup granulated sugar

2 tsp vanilla

Grease a shallow 6 to 7 cup baking dish.

Spread bread slices with butter and then jam. Arrange, slightly overlapping, in a single layer in prepared dish. Sprinkle with remaining raisins.

Whisk remaining ingredients in large bowl. Pour over bread and let stand for 15 minutes.

Preheat oven to 350°F (180°C). Scatter half of raisins over bottom of dish.

Place baking dish in roasting pan and pour enough hot water into roasting pan to come halfway up sides of baking dish. Bake in preheated oven for about 1 hour or until center is set. Let stand for 15 minutes before serving.

Do-ahead tips: *You can make this 2 days ahead. Serve cold or cover with foil and reheat in 325°F (160°C) oven for 15 to 20 minutes.*

Cinnamon Scrolls

These are best served warm although they can be made a day ahead and reheated in microwave for about 20 seconds each. When making dough it is always best to start with a little less flour and add more as needed.

⅔ cup warm milk

2 tsp active dry yeast

2 eggs, at room temperature

¼ cup granulated sugar

2½ –3 cups all purpose flour

½ tsp salt

⅓ cup butter, melted

Cinnamon Filling

½ cup butter, softened

½ cup packed brown sugar

2 tsp ground cinnamon

⅔ cup (3 oz/90 g) ground almonds (almond meal)

Lightly grease muffin pans (18 holes needed).

Whisk milk, yeast, eggs and sugar in medium bowl until well combined.

Combine flour and salt in large bowl; make well in center. Add milk mixture and butter and stir until mixture forms a soft dough. Turn onto lightly floured surface and knead for 5 to 10 minutes or until smooth and elastic.

Place dough in lightly oiled bowl; turn to coat in oil. Cover with greased plastic wrap and clean tea towel and let stand in warm place for about 1½ hours or until dough is doubled in size.

Roll out dough on lightly floured surface to 18 x 10 inch (45 x 25 cm) rectangle with one long side closest to you. Spread filling evenly over dough, leaving a 1 inch (2.5 cm) border along top long side. Starting with long side closest to you, roll up dough to enclose filling. Cut into 18, 1 inch (2.5 cm) pieces. Place each piece, cut side up, in lightly greased muffin pans. Cover with greased plastic wrap and clean tea towels, and let stand in warm place for 45 minutes or until risen. Preheat oven to 350°F (180°C). Bake on center rack for 20 to 25 minutes or until golden brown.

Cinnamon Filling: Combine all ingredients in small bowl until well mixed.

Bacon and Herb Breakfast Bake

This dish is delicious served warm and drizzled with maple syrup. It needs to be prepared a day ahead of baking.

8 slices bacon, chopped

2 tsp canola oil

1 cup chopped onion

1 cup chopped red pepper

10 slices bread, cut into 1 inch (2.5 cm) cubes

8 eggs

4 cups milk

1/4 cup mayonnaise

3 Tbsp Dijon mustard

3 Tbsp chopped fresh parsley

2 Tbsp chopped fresh chives

1/4 tsp salt

1/4 tsp coarsely ground pepper

Lightly grease a 10 to 12 cup baking dish that has 3 to 3½ inch (8 to 9 cm) sides. Preheat oven to 350°F (180°C).

Cook bacon in large frying pan over medium heat until golden brown. Place on paper towel. Drain fat from pan. Heat oil in same pan over medium heat and add onion, pepper and bacon. Cook for about 5 minutes or until onion is softened.

Place bread in prepared baking dish. Scatter onion mixture over bread.

Whisk remaining ingredients in large bowl; pour over bread. Cover and refrigerate for 8 hours or overnight.

Let stand at room temperature for 1 hour before baking. Cook in preheated oven for about 1 hour or until set and golden brown.

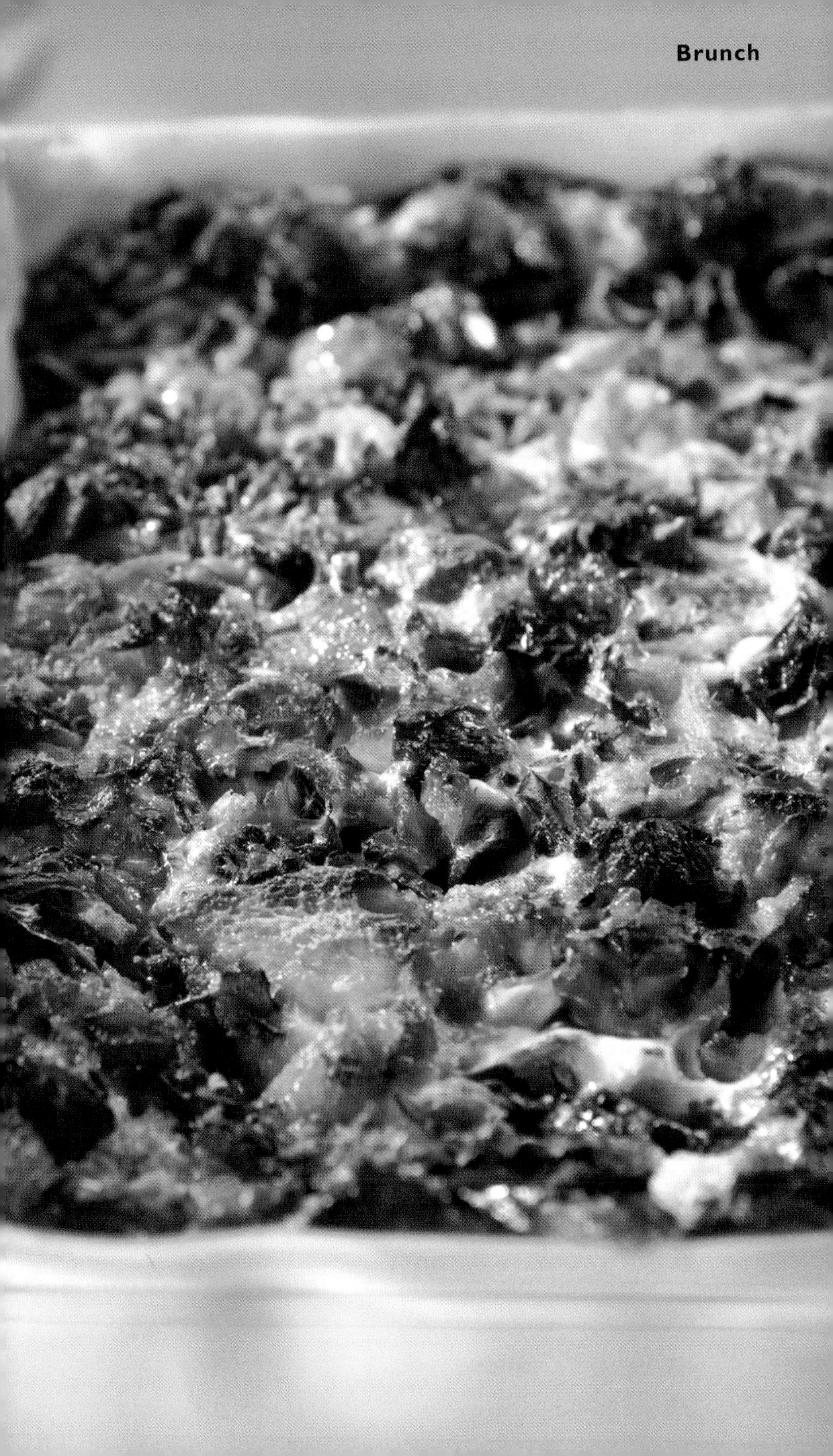

Chocolate Truffles

It is best to use a good quality chocolate. It is easier to work with and the results are better.

Lime Coconut Truffles

- ¼ cup whipping cream
- ¼ cup butter
- 5 oz (200 g) white chocolate, chopped
- 2 Tbsp coconut-flavored liqueur (e.g., Malibu)
- 1 Tbsp finely grated lime rind
- 6½ oz (200 g) white chocolate, melted
- 1¼ cups medium unsweetened coconut, toasted (see p. 7)

Cherry Chocolate Truffles

- ¼ cup brandy
- ½ cup (4 oz/125 g) red glazed cherries, finely chopped
- ¼ cup whipping cream
- ¼ cup butter
- 6½ oz (200 g) dark chocolate, chopped
- 6½ oz (200 g) milk chocolate, melted (see p. 6)
- extra chopped cherries for decorating

Do-ahead tips: *These can be made a week ahead and kept in a sealed container in the refrigerator.*

Lime Coconut Truffles (makes about 30): Stir cream and butter in small saucepan on medium-high heat until butter is melted; remove from heat. Add chopped white chocolate and stir until melted.

Add liqueur and rind and stir. Scrape mixture into small bowl. Chill for 1 to 2 hours, stirring occasionally, or until mixture is thick but not hard.

Drop rounded teaspoons of mixture onto foil-lined baking sheet. Chill for about 1 hour or until firm enough to roll into balls. Do not overchill or balls will be too hard to roll. Roll into balls and place on same baking sheet; chill for 30 minutes. To make rolling easier, wipe hands with dry cloth such as a paper towel to remove chocolate in between rolling balls.

Dip each ball in melted white chocolate then into coconut and place on foil-lined baking sheet and chill until firm.

Cherry Chocolate Truffles (makes about 35): Combine brandy and cherries in small bowl and let stand for 15 minutes.

Stir cream and butter in small saucepan on medium-high

heat until butter is melted; remove from heat. Add dark chocolate and stir until melted.

Stir in cherry mixture. Scrape mixture into small bowl. Chill for 1 to 2 hours, stirring occasionally, or until mixture is thick but not hard.

Drop rounded teaspoons of mixture onto foil-lined baking sheet; chill for about 1 hour or until firm enough to roll into balls. Do not overchill or balls will be too hard to roll. Roll into balls and place on same baking sheet; chill for 30 minutes. To make rolling easier, wipe hands with dry cloth such as a paper towel to remove chocolate in between rolling balls.

Dip each ball in melted milk chocolate and place on foil-lined baking sheet. Top with a piece of extra cherry before chocolate sets; chill.

Christmas Pudding with Two Sauces

This delicious pudding is steamed. Pudding steamers can be found in kitchen specialty stores.

1 cup (6 oz/185 g) dark raisins

1 cup (6 oz/185 g) golden raisins

1 cup (6 oz/185 g) dates, pitted, chopped

1 cup (6 oz/185 g) pitted prunes, chopped

½ cup (4 oz/125 g) mixed peel

1 cup water

1 cup packed brown sugar

½ cup butter

1 tsp baking soda

2 eggs, lightly beaten

3 Tbsp brandy

2 cups all purpose flour

2 tsp baking powder

½ tsp ground cinnamon

½ tsp ground nutmeg

¼ tsp ground cloves

Hard Sauce

1 cup butter, softened

1¾ cups icing sugar

¼ cup orange-flavored liqueur (e.g., Cointreau)

1 tsp finely grated orange rind

Warm Brandy Sauce

1 cup granulated sugar

¼ cup water

½ cup whipping cream

¼ cup brandy

2 Tbsp butter

Grease an 8 cup pudding steamer and line base with parchment paper. Combine dried fruits, water, sugar and butter in large saucepan. Stir over medium heat until sugar is dissolved and butter is melted. Bring to boil then reduce heat to medium-low. Simmer, uncovered, for 7 minutes. Remove from heat and immediately stir in baking soda; cool.

Add eggs and stir until well combined.

Sift flour, baking powder and spices into pudding mixture and stir until well combined. Spoon into prepared pudding steamer and smooth top. Cover steamer with parchment paper, then foil, allowing parchment paper and foil to come 1 to 2 inches (2.5 to 5 cm) over edge. Tie string around rim of steamer, securing paper and foil.

Place small heat-resistant plate on bottom of stock pot. Place steamer on plate. Add enough boiling water to come halfway up side of steamer. Cover pot with tight-fitting lid. Boil for 5 hours, adding more water when necessary.

Let stand for 20 minutes before turning out. Cut into 8 wedges. Serve warm with Hard Sauce and warm Brandy Sauce.

Hard Sauce: Beat butter and icing sugar in small bowl with electric mixer for 5 to 10 minutes or until light and fluffy. Add liqueur and rind and beat until well combined. Spoon into a 2 cup serving dish, cover; chill until set. Makes about 2 cups.

Warm Brandy Sauce: Stir sugar and water in small saucepan over medium heat until sugar is dissolved. Boil

gently, without stirring, for about 5 minutes
until mixture turns a pale golden color.
Stir in cream carefully as mixture
may bubble up. Add brandy and
stir until mixture is hot but
not boiling. Remove from
heat and add butter.
Stir until melted.
Serve warm.

Do-ahead tips: *The pudding can be made 1 month
ahead wrapped in plastic wrap and foil and stored in
the refrigerator. To reheat pudding, cut into wedges,
cover and microwave on 100% power for 30 seconds or
until warm. Or, place whole pudding into a greased
pudding steamer, cover with tight-fitting lid or
foil and boil for 1 hour or until hot.*

Fruit Cake

This dark fruit cake does not contain eggs and is sweetened with condensed milk, making it moist and delicious. The fruit can be soaked in rum 1 month ahead of time.

2 cups (12 oz/375 g) dark raisins

2 cups (12 oz/375 g) pitted dates, chopped

1 cup (6 oz/185 g) pitted prunes, chopped

1 cup (6 oz/185 g) golden raisins

1 cup (8 oz/250 g) red glazed cherries, halved

2/3 cup (5 oz/150 g) chopped glazed pineapple

1/3 cup (2 oz/60 g) mixed peel

3/4 cup spiced rum, plus another 1/3 cup

1 cup water

1 cup butter, cubed

10 oz (300 ml) can sweetened condensed milk

2 cups all purpose flour

1 tsp ground ginger

1/2 tsp ground cinnamon

1/2 tsp ground nutmeg

1 tsp baking powder

1 tsp baking soda

1/3 cup (1 oz/30 g) pecan halves

12 red glazed cherries, halved

12 green glazed cherries, halved

1/3 cup spiced rum, plus extra for drizzling

Line a deep 9 inch (22 cm) round pan with 3 layers of parchment paper, ensuring paper comes 2 inches (5 cm) up side of pan.

Combine all dried and glazed fruit and peel with 3/4 cup of rum in large bowl. Cover and let stand at least 12 hours, stirring occasionally. Spoon into large saucepan.

Add water and butter. Stir over medium-high heat until butter is melted. Simmer, uncovered, stirring occasionally, for 5 minutes. Spoon into extra large bowl; cool.

Stir in condensed milk.

Preheat oven to 300°F (150°C).

Combine flour, spices, baking powder and baking soda in medium bowl. Add to fruit mixture and mix well. Spread mixture into prepared pan; knock bottom of pan on solid surface to remove any air pockets in cake. Smooth top of cake.

Arrange pecans and cherries in decorative pattern over top of cake. Bake in preheated oven for 2½ to 3 hours or until firm and a thin blade knife inserted into center of cake comes out clean—knife may be a little bit sticky from fruit. Cover cake loosely with brown paper or foil during cooking if top is over-browning.

Drizzle extra rum over cake. Cover with foil and let cool in pan. When completely cool, turn cake out and wrap well in plastic wrap then in foil. To serve, cut cake into 1 inch (2.5 cm) thick slices, then cut each slice into 2 inch (5 cm) wide pieces.

Do-ahead tips: *Wrap cake well in plastic wrap and foil and store in a sealed container for up to 3 months. It can also be frozen for up to 6 months.*

Walnut Pie with Cranberry Cream

Tart pans are available at kitchen stores.

Pie Crust

- 1 cup all purpose flour
- 2 Tbsp granulated sugar
- $1/2$ cup butter
- 1 egg, lightly beaten

Walnut Filling

- 3 eggs
- 1 cup packed brown sugar
- 1 cup golden corn syrup
- $1/4$ cup butter, melted
- 1 tsp vanilla
- $1/4$ tsp salt
- $1/4$ tsp ground cinnamon
- 2 cups walnuts, toasted (see p. 7), coarsely chopped

Cranberry Cream

- 1 cup whipping cream
- $1/3$ cup cranberry jelly room temperature
- 1 to 2 Tbsp orange-flavored liqueur (e.g., Cointreau)
- $1/4$ tsp ground cinnamon

Pie Crust: Place flour and sugar in large bowl and rub in butter until mixture resembles coarse crumbs. Add egg and stir until a soft dough forms.

Turn dough onto lightly floured surface and knead very lightly just until dough is smooth. Roll pastry until large enough to fit into non-greased 10 inch (25 cm) tart pan; cover with plastic wrap. Place on baking sheet. Chill for 1 hour.

Line pastry with parchment paper and half fill with dried beans or rice. Bake on bottom shelf of preheated oven for 15 minutes. Remove paper and beans. Cool pastry.

Walnut Filling: Whisk all ingredients except walnuts in medium bowl until smooth. Stir in walnuts.

Pour filling into cooled pastry shell; smooth top. Bake on bottom shelf of preheated oven for 35 to 40 minutes or until firm. Filling may be a little wobbly in center but will set on cooling. Place on wire rack to cool. This pie can be served warm or cold.

Cranberry Cream: Whip cream in medium bowl until soft peaks form. Fold in remaining ingredients.

Cashew and Apricot Chocolate Bark

For best results use a good quality chocolate such as Callebaut or Lindt.

1 lb (500 g) milk chocolate, melted (see p. 6)

1 cup (5 oz/150 g) cashew nuts, toasted (see p. 7), coarsely chopped

½ cup (2½ oz/75 g) finely chopped dried apricots

1 Tbsp finely grated orange rind

Line a baking sheet with parchment paper. Combine all ingredients in large bowl. Spread thinly onto prepared baking sheet and let stand until cool. Refrigerate until firm.

Break into 2 inch (5 cm) pieces.

Do-ahead tips: *This can be made a week ahead and stored in a sealed container in refrigerator.*

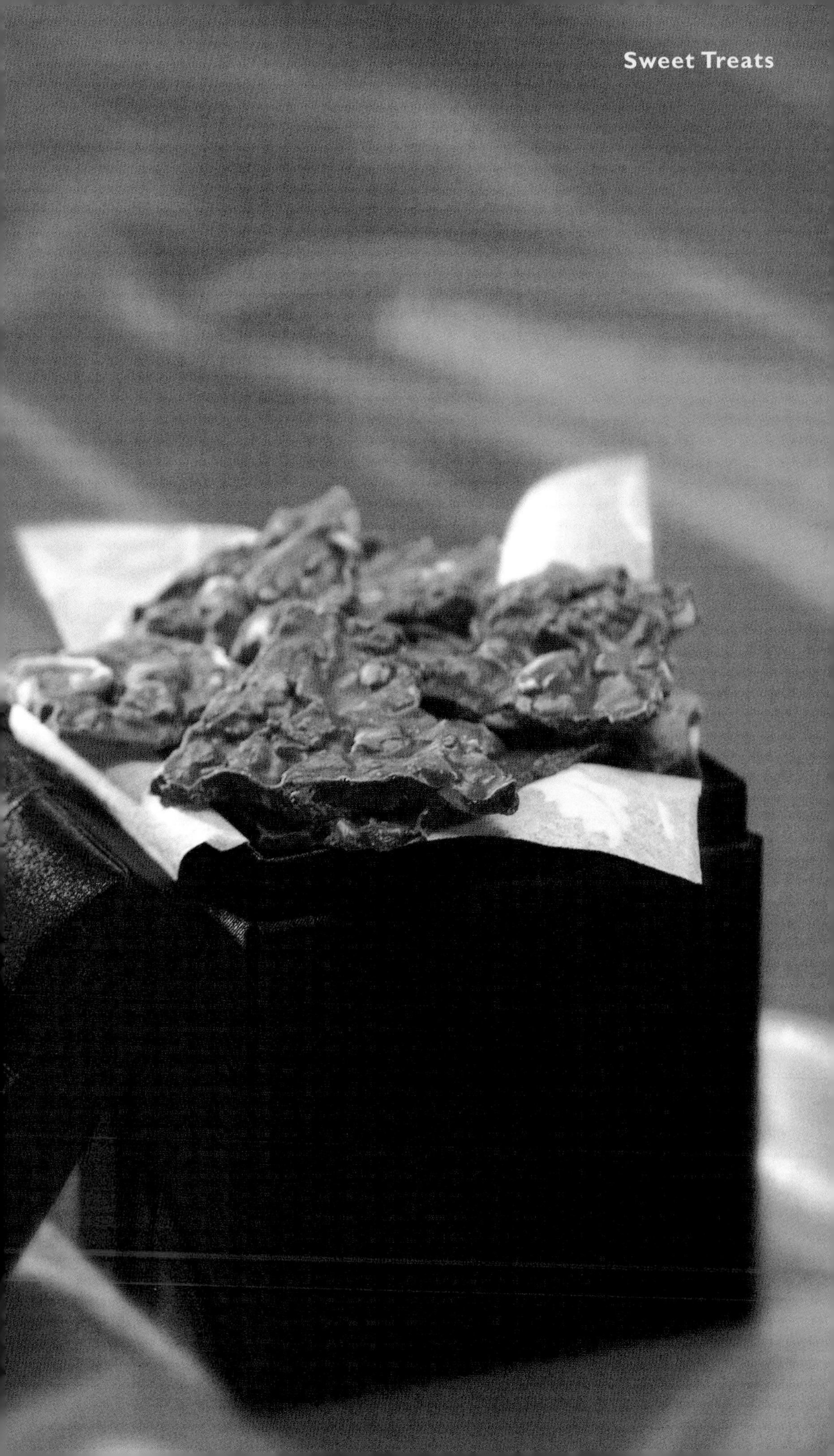

Ginger Chocolate Biscotti

This hard Italian-style biscuit is best served with coffee for dunking.

1½ cups all purpose flour

3 Tbsp cocoa powder

½ tsp baking powder

⅔ cup granulated sugar, plus another 2 tsp

¼ cup butter, softened

2 eggs

½ tsp vanilla

½ cup (3½ oz/115 g) crystallized ginger, finely chopped

1 egg white, lightly beaten

Grease a baking sheet. Preheat oven to 350°F (180°C).

Place flour, cocoa, baking powder and ⅔ cup of sugar in food processor. Process until mixed. Add butter and process until well combined.

Add eggs and vanilla and process until mixture forms a smooth dough.

Place dough on lightly floured surface and knead in ginger.

Divide dough into 2 equal portions and shape into logs about 8 inches (20 cm) long. Place diagonally, about 2 to 3 inches (5 to 8 cm) apart on prepared baking sheet.

Brush with egg white, then sprinkle with extra 2 teaspoons of sugar. Bake in preheated oven for about 30 minutes or until cracked across top and firm. Let stand for 15 minutes before transferring to cutting board. Reduce the oven temperature to 325°F (160°C).

Cut diagonally into ½ inch (1.2 cm) thick slices. Place each slice, cut side up, on baking sheets. Bake for about 30 minutes until dry and crisp. Cool on wire racks.

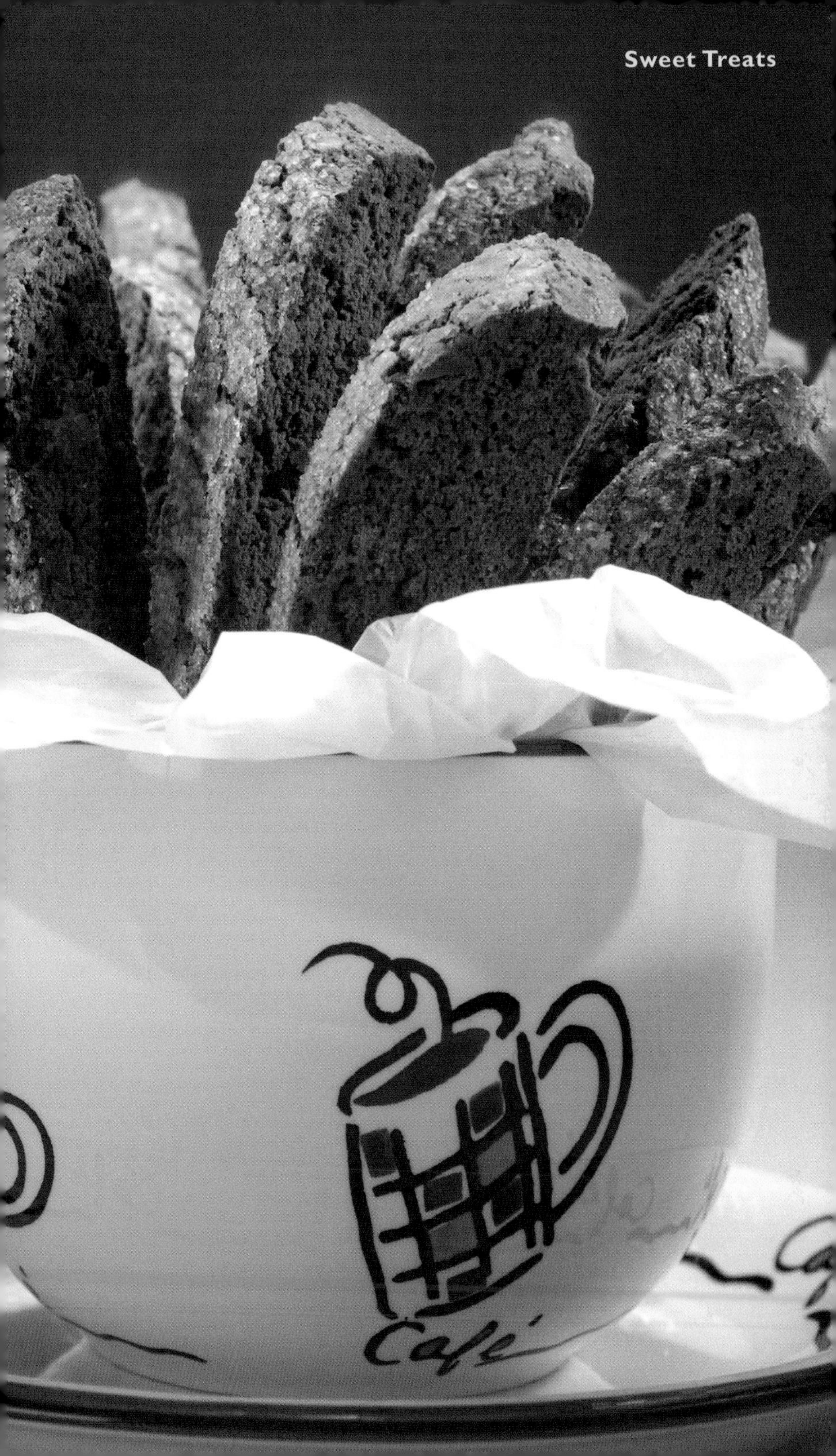
Café

Gingerbread Men

Meringue powder can be found in kitchen specialty stores. Paste and powder food colorings will give a deeper, more intense color than liquid colorings.

1 cup butter, softened
1 cup packed brown sugar
1 egg
1 cup fancy molasses
2 Tbsp milk
5 cups all purpose flour
1½ tsp baking soda
1 Tbsp ground ginger
1 tsp ground cinnamon
¼ tsp ground cloves
pinch of salt
gold dragees (small edible beads)

icing

1 cup icing sugar
3 Tbsp meringue powder
2 to 3 Tbsp water, approximately
red food coloring (paste)
brown food coloring (paste)
gold dragees (small edible candy beads), optional

Line cookie sheets with parchment paper. Preheat oven to 350°F (180°C).

Beat butter and sugar in large bowl of heavy-duty mixer until well combined and sugar is dissolved. Add egg, molasses and milk and beat until well combined.

Sift flour, baking soda, spices and salt into large bowl. Add to butter mixture in 3 batches and beat until smooth dough forms.

Divide dough in half. Cover 1 portion with plastic wrap and set aside. Roll 1 portion onto lightly floured surface until ¼ inch (6 mm) thickness. Cut out shapes using 5 inch (13 cm) cookie cutter.

Place gingerbread men 1½ inches (3.8 cm) apart on prepared cookie sheets. Bake in preheated oven for about 15 minutes or until just firm and starting to brown around edges. Let stand on cookie sheets for 10 minutes before transferring to wire racks to cool completely. Repeat with remaining dough. Off-cuts of uncooked dough can be re-rolled and cut out.

icing Place icing sugar and meringue powder in small bowl and add enough water to mix to a fairly thick paste. Separate icing into 2 small bowls and color one with red food coloring and other with brown coloring. Place each icing in 2 small piping bags fitted with plain tip. Decorate gingerbread men as desired. Place dragees on icing while still wet. Let stand for 30 minutes or until icing is set completely before storing.

Do ahead tip: Gingerbread men can be made 1 week ahead and stored in sealed containers in a cool, dry place.

Cinnamon Shortbread

This is a shortbread pastry, so you may find some cracking as you roll and shape the dough; just gently press any cracks together. Omit the cinnamon for a plain shortbread if desired.

2 cups butter, softened
1 cup granulated sugar
4 cups all purpose flour
1 cup white rice flour
1 tsp ground cinnamon, optional
¼ tsp salt

Grease 2 large baking sheets. Preheat oven to 325°F (160°C).

Beat butter and sugar in medium bowl with electric mixer until well combined.

Stir both flours, cinnamon and salt in medium bowl. Add to butter mixture in 3 batches, beating between each addition until well combined.

Turn onto lightly floured surface. Press together to form a soft dough. Divide dough into 4 portions. Cover 3 portions with plastic wrap and set aside.

Roll 1 portion into 7 inch (18 cm) round disk. Carefully lift onto prepared baking sheet. With a sharp knife mark top into 8 even wedges and prick all over with fork. Create a decorative edge by pinching the pastry around the edge with lightly floured fingers. Repeat with remaining dough.

Two disks will fit onto each large baking sheet about 1 to 2 inches (2.5 to 5 cm) apart. Bake in preheated oven for about 30 minutes until very lightly golden. Let stand for 10 minutes before carefully transferring to wire racks to cool.

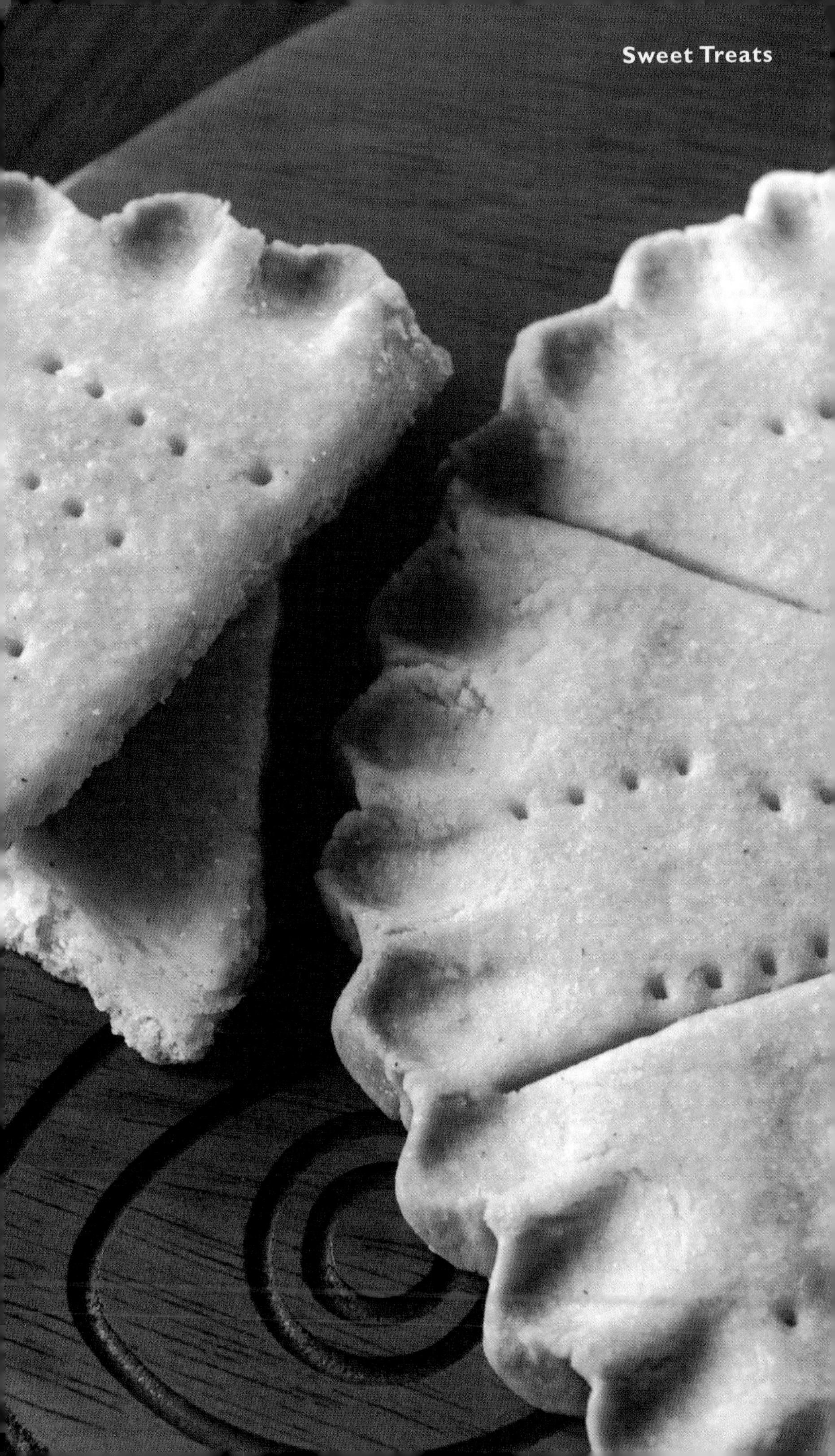

Strawberry Chocolate Trifle

For best results, trifle must be made a day ahead.

2 x 2³/₄ oz (85 g) packages strawberry-flavored gelatin

³/₄ cup orange juice

¹/₂ cup orange-flavored liqueur (e.g., Cointreau) or orange juice

2 x 4 oz (125 g) packages lady finger biscuits

2 baskets strawberries, hulled and sliced

1¹/₂ cups whipping cream

¹/₂ cup strawberry jam, room temperature

3¹/₂ oz (100 g) dark chocolate, coarsely grated

Chocolate Sauce

¹/₂ cup whipping cream

7¹/₂ oz (200 g) dark chocolate, chopped

¹/₂ cup small white marshmallows

Prepare jelly according to directions on packages. Pour both into same shallow dish and refrigerate for about 3 hours until set. Cut into ¹/₂ inch (1.2 cm) cubes.

Combine juice and liqueur in small bowl. Dip half of biscuits into juice mixture and place over bottom and part way up side of 14 to 16 cup trifle dish.

Spoon half of jelly over biscuits.

Beat whipping cream in medium bowl until soft peaks form; fold in jam.

Spoon half of strawberries over jelly, spread with half of Chocolate Sauce then spread with half of cream mixture.

Dip remaining biscuits in remaining juice mixture and layer over cream mixture. Spoon remaining jelly over biscuits.

Spoon remaining strawberries over jelly, spread remaining sauce over strawberries and spread with remaining cream mixture. Cover and refrigerate for 8 hours or overnight.

Sprinkle top with grated chocolate just before serving.

Chocolate Sauce: Heat cream in medium saucepan over medium-high heat until bubbling. Remove from heat and stir in chocolate and marshmallows. Stir until chocolate and marshmallows are melted.

Butter Tarts

Make these to give away during the festive season or add them to a platter of sweets to serve family and friends.

2 x 8 oz (255 g) packages mini tart shells (2 inch/5 cm size)

⅔ cup (3½ oz/110 g) dark raisins

2 tsp finely grated orange rind

⅓ cup orange juice

1¾ cups packed brown sugar

¾ cup butter

¼ cup whipping cream

2 tsp white vinegar

1 tsp vanilla

¼ tsp salt

3 eggs, lightly beaten

Place tart shells on 2 baking sheets. Preheat oven to 375°F (190°C).

Combine raisins, rind and juice in small bowl. Let stand for 20 minutes.

Heat sugar, butter, cream, vinegar, vanilla and salt in medium saucepan over medium heat and stir until sugar is dissolved; let cool.

Add eggs and stir until well combined.

Drain raisins and discard liquid. Divide raisins among tart shells. Spoon 2 teaspoons of brown sugar mixture into each tart shell. Bake on bottom shelf of preheated oven for about 25 minutes or until pastry is golden and filling is bubbling. Cool on baking sheets for 5 minutes before transferring to wire racks. Serve cold or warm.

Rum Balls

These can dry out, so they are best eaten within 1 to 2 days of making.

8 oz (250 g) package vanilla-flavored wafers

1 cup granulated sugar

¼ cup golden corn syrup

½ cup spiced rum

6½ oz (200 g) dark chocolate, chopped

1½ cups chocolate sprinkles, approximately

Line baking sheet with foil. Place wafers in food processor and process until mixture resembles fine crumbs.

Heat sugar, syrup and rum in medium saucepan over medium-low heat and stir until sugar is dissolved; do not boil. Remove from heat.

Add chocolate and stir until melted. Add wafer crumbs and stir until well combined.

Drop 2-teaspoon mounds of mixture onto prepared baking sheets. Roll each mound into a ball, using lightly moistened hands. If mixture is not thick enough to roll, place in refrigerator for 5 to 10 minutes.

Place sprinkles on waxed paper or in shallow dish. Roll each ball into sprinkles while still moist. Place on same baking sheet and chill for 1 hour or until firm. Place into sealed containers and store in refrigerator. Remove from refrigerator about 1 hour before serving.

Do-ahead tips: *Can be made 1 to 2 days ahead and stored in a sealed container in refrigerator.*

Pumpkin Tart with a Ginger Crust

This tart is best served cold.

8 oz (250 g) ginger cookies
1/3 cup (1 oz/30 g) pecans
1/2 cup butter, melted

Filling

3 eggs
1/3 cup packed brown sugar
1/4 cup maple syrup
14 oz (398 ml) can pure pumpkin
2/3 cup evaporated milk
1/2 tsp ground cinnamon
1/2 tsp ground ginger
1/4 tsp ground nutmeg
1/8 tsp salt
icing sugar for dusting

Place cookies and pecans in food processor and process until fine crumbs. Combine butter and crumb mixture in medium bowl.

Using a flat-bottom, straight-sided glass, press mixture into non-greased 10 inch (25 cm) tart pan with removable base. Place on baking sheet. Chill for 30 minutes.

Do-ahead tips: *Tart is best made a day ahead. Store in a sealed container in the refrigerator.*

Filling: Preheat oven to 350°F (180°C).

With electric mixer, beat eggs, sugar and syrup in large bowl until thick and pale.

Add remaining ingredients and beat until well combined.

Pour into prepared crust and smooth top. Bake in preheated oven for about 45 minutes or until filling is set. Refrigerate for 6 hours or overnight before serving. Dust with icing sugar just before serving if desired.

Ginger and Date Cake with Toffee Rum Sauce

This decadent, wintery dessert is sure to become a favorite.

Ginger and Date Cake

- 1 cup (6 oz/185 g) dates, pitted, coarsely chopped
- 1 cup water
- 1 tsp baking soda
- 1/3 cup butter, softened
- 1 cup packed brown sugar
- 2 eggs
- 1 1/4 cups all purpose flour
- 2 tsp baking powder
- 1/2 cup (3 1/2 oz/115 g) crystallized ginger, chopped

Toffee Rum Sauce

- 1/2 cup butter
- 1/2 cup packed brown sugar
- 1/2 cup whipping cream
- 1/4 cup spiced rum

Ginger and Date Cake: Grease an 8 inch (20 cm) springform pan and line base and side with parchment paper. Preheat oven to 350°F (180°C).

Combine dates and water in medium saucepan on medium-high heat. Bring to boil then remove from heat and add baking soda (mixture will bubble up); cool.

Beat butter, sugar and eggs in medium bowl with an electric mixer until well combined.

Sift flour and baking powder into butter mixture. Add date mixture and ginger and beat until well combined.

Scrape mixture into prepared pan. Bake in preheated oven for 55 to 60 minutes or until skewer inserted in center comes out clean. Let cool in pan for 10 minutes before transferring to wire rack. Serve warm or cold with warm Toffee Rum Sauce.

Toffee Rum Sauce: Combine all ingredients in medium saucepan over medium heat until sugar is dissolved and butter is melted. Let boil without stirring for 3 minutes. Remove from heat and stir in rum.

Do-ahead tips: *Cake and sauce can be made a day ahead and reheated in microwave until warm.*

White Chocolate and Cranberry Cookies

Fill your cookie jar with these yummy cookies or package them and give them away as gifts.

1 egg
¾ cup packed brown sugar
¼ cup granulated sugar
½ cup canola oil
1 tsp vanilla
1 cup all purpose flour
½ tsp baking powder
¼ tsp salt
8 oz (225 g) package white chocolate chips
¾ cup (4 oz/125 g) dried cranberries

Line cookie sheets with parchment paper.

Beat egg and both sugars in small bowl with an electric mixer until pale and creamy.

Add oil and vanilla and stir until combined. Sift flour, baking powder and salt into sugar mixture and stir.

Add chocolate and cranberries and mix well. Cover and refrigerate for 30 minutes.

Preheat oven to 350°F (180°C).

Roll rounded tablespoons of mixture into balls. Place on prepared cookie sheets about 3 inches (7.5 cm) apart. Bake in preheated oven for about 12 minutes or until golden. Let stand on cookie sheets for 5 minutes before transferring to wire rack to cool. Cool completely before storing.

Chocolate Dessert Cake

Remove cake from refrigerator at least 1 hour before serving. This cake is delicious served with ice cream or whipped cream.

9½ oz (300 g) dark chocolate, chopped
1 cup butter
¾ cup packed brown sugar
3 Tbsp coffee-flavored liqueur (e.g., Kahlua)
2 Tbsp prepared strong black coffee
1 cup all purpose flour
¼ cup cocoa powder
½ tsp baking powder
2 eggs, lightly beaten
extra cocoa for dusting

Fudge Icing

3 Tbsp butter
2 Tbsp water
¼ cup granulated sugar
¾ cup icing sugar
3 Tbsp cocoa powder

Grease base and side of 9 inch (22 cm) springform pan and line base and side with parchment paper. Preheat oven to 325°F (160°C).

Stir chocolate, butter, sugar, liqueur and coffee in large saucepan over low heat until chocolate and butter are melted and sugar is dissolved; cool.

Add remaining ingredients and whisk until well combined and smooth. Pour mixture into prepared pan. Bake in preheated oven for 1 to 1¼ hours or until skewer inserted in center comes out clean. Let cool in pan.

Do-ahead tips: *Cake can be made 3 to 5 days ahead and stored, well covered, in refrigerator.*

Remove from pan. Spread cooled cake with Fudge Icing. Cover and refrigerate for 6 hours or overnight. Dust with cocoa if desired.

Fudge Icing: Stir butter, water and granulated sugar in small saucepan over medium heat until sugar is dissolved.

Add icing sugar and cocoa and stir until smooth. Scrape into small bowl. Cover and refrigerate for about 1 hour or until thickened and spreadable.

White Chocolate and Coffee Cheesecake

A truly decadent dessert flavored with almond liqueur, this is sure to be a popular addition to any festive feast.

8 oz (250 g) package vanilla-flavored wafers

1 cup (2½ oz/80 g) sliced almonds, toasted (see p. 7)

½ cup butter, melted

Filling

½ cup prepared strong black coffee

1 envelope unflavored gelatin

2 x 8 oz (250 g) packages cream cheese, softened

½ cup granulated sugar

¼ cup almond-flavored liqueur (e.g., Amaretto)

13 oz (400 g) white chocolate, melted (see p. 6)

1 cup whipping cream

10 to 12 chocolate-coated coffee beans

Grease base and side of 9 inch (22 cm) springform pan and line with parchment paper.

Process wafers and almonds in food processor until fine crumbs. Add butter and process until well combined. Scrape mixture into prepared pan. Using a flat-bottom, straight-sided glass, press mixture over base and three-quarters way up side of pan. Refrigerate for 30 minutes.

Filling: Place coffee in small saucepan; sprinkle gelatin over coffee. Stir on low heat until gelatin is dissolved; cool slightly.

Beat cream cheese, sugar and liqueur in large bowl with electric mixer until smooth.

Add chocolate and gelatin mixture and beat until well

Do-ahead tips: *Cheesecake is best made a day ahead, but it can be made 3 days ahead.*

combined. Scrape into crust and smooth top. Cover and refrigerate for 8 hours or overnight.

Beat whipping cream in small bowl with electric mixer until soft peaks form. Spread cream over cheesecake. Arrange coffee beans around top. Carefully run knife around outer edge of cheesecake before removing ring from pan.

Apple Pie with Streusel Walnut Topping

This is a slight twist on an old favorite, using a streusel mixture in place of a pastry top.

1¼ cups all purpose flour

⅓ cup cold butter, chopped

¼ cup icing sugar

2 egg yolks

1 Tbsp iced water

⅛ tsp salt

10 medium green apples, peeled, cored, coarsely chopped

1 cup granulated sugar

½ cup water

Streusel Walnut Topping

1 cup all purpose flour

2 tsp baking powder

½ cup cold butter, chopped

1 cup packed brown sugar

½ cup (2 oz/60 g) walnuts, toasted (see p. 7), chopped

Grease a 9 inch (22 cm) pie plate.

Place flour in large bowl and cut in butter until well combined; stir in sugar. Add egg yolks and enough iced water to mix to soft dough.

Roll dough out on lightly floured surface until ⅛ inch (3 mm) thickness. Place in prepared pie plate and trim and crimp edge. Cover with plastic wrap and refrigerate for 1 hour.

Combine apples, sugar and water in large saucepan. Bring to boil then reduce to medium heat. Simmer, covered, stirring occasionally, for about 10 minutes or until apples are tender. Drain well and let cool.

Preheat oven to 375°F (180°C).

Spoon cooled apple mixture into pastry shell. Sprinkle with Streusel Walnut Topping. Bake, on bottom rack, in preheated oven for about 50 minutes or until base is browned. Cover loosely with foil during cooking if top is over-browning. Let stand for 15 minutes before cutting.

Streusel Walnut Topping: Combine flour and baking powder in medium bowl. Rub in butter until mixture resembles coarse crumbs. Stir in sugar and walnuts and stir until well combined.

Do-ahead tips: *Pie can be made a day ahead and served cold. Or, have pastry shell ready and in pie plate, have the apples cooked and the Streusel Walnut Topping ready a day ahead and store covered in refrigerator. Remove from refrigerator 1 to 3 hours before assembling and baking. All you have to do is spoon apples into pastry and sprinkle with topping and bake.*

Sugar Cookies

Cut out and decorate cookies in the shapes and colors you desire.

¾ cup butter, softened

1 cup granulated sugar

⅓ cup sour cream

1 egg

1 tsp vanilla

2¾ cups all purpose flour

1 tsp baking powder

¼ tsp baking soda

¼ tsp salt

1 egg white, lightly beaten

pink colored sugar

green colored sugar

Icing

1 cup icing sugar

3 Tbsp meringue powder

2 to 3 Tbsp water, approximately

green food coloring (paste)

red food coloring (paste)

silver dragees (small edible candy balls)

Line cookie sheets with parchment paper.

Beat butter, sugar, sour cream, egg and vanilla in large bowl with electric mixer until well combined and sugar is dissolved.

Combine flour, baking power, baking soda and salt in medium bowl. Add to butter mixture in three additions. Beat until a soft dough forms. Turn dough onto lightly floured surface. Knead lightly until smooth. Divide dough in half and wrap each half in plastic wrap and refrigerate for 30 minutes.

Preheat oven to 375°F (190°C).

Roll dough on lightly floured surface until ¼ inch (6 mm) thickness. Cut out shapes using cutter of your choice lightly dipped in flour. Place on prepared cookie sheets about 1 inch (2.5 cm) apart.

Brush half of cookies with egg white, then sprinkle with colored sugar. Bake in preheated oven for about 8 minutes or until edges of cookies are starting to lightly brown. Let stand on cookie sheets for 5 minutes before transferring to wire rack to cool completely.

Decorate remaining cookies with icing and dragees. Let stand until icing is set before storing.

Icing: Place sugar and meringue powder in small bowl and add enough water to mix to fairly thick paste. Place half of icing into another small bowl. Color one icing pink and other green. Spoon each icing into piping bags fitted with plain small tips. Pipe icing onto cookies and decorate with dragees as desired.

Cherry Pie

This must be the easiest pie in the world to make. The almond flavoring gives the pie a wonderful, unique taste. The pie is best served cold the day after it is prepared and is delicious with ice cream or custard.

Pie Crust

- 1 cup all purpose flour
- 3 Tbsp granulated sugar
- 1/2 cup butter, softened

Filling

- 2 eggs
- 1 cup granulated sugar
- 1/3 cup all purpose flour
- 1 tsp almond flavoring
- 1/2 tsp baking powder
- 1/4 tsp salt
- 14 fl oz (398 ml) can pitted cherries, drained

Pie Crust: Grease a 9 inch (22 cm) pie dish. Preheat oven to 325°F (160°C).

Combine flour and sugar in medium bowl. Rub in butter until well combined. Press pastry into bottom and up side of prepared pie dish. Bake on bottom rack in preheated oven for 20 minutes.

Filling: Whisk all ingredients except cherries in medium bowl. Stir in cherries and pour into pastry shell. Pastry does not need to cool before adding filling.

Bake on bottom rack in preheated oven for 1 to 1¼ hours or until pastry is browned and filling is set. Cool before covering and storing in refrigerator.

Dust with icing sugar before serving if desired.

Do-ahead tips: *Pie is best made a day ahead.*

Lemon Curd and Cranberry Baked Cheesecake

This dessert needs to be made a day ahead.

⅔ cup (3½ oz/110 g) dried cranberries

⅓ cup lemon juice

8 oz (250 g) package vanilla-flavored wafers

1 cup (4 oz/125 g) walnuts

⅔ cup butter, melted

3 eggs

⅔ cup granulated sugar

2 x 8 oz (250 g) packages cream cheese, softened

2 Tbsp finely grated lemon rind

Lemon Curd Topping

1 cup butter

¾ cup granulated sugar

⅔ cup lemon juice

3 eggs

Grease a 9 inch (22 cm) springform pan and line base and side with parchment paper.

Combine cranberries and juice in small bowl and let stand for 30 minutes.

Meanwhile, place wafers and walnuts in food processor or blender and process until mixture resembles fine crumbs; transfer to medium bowl.

Add butter and stir until well combined. Press mixture into prepared pan using a flat-bottom, straight-sided glass until mixture comes two-thirds up side of pan. Chill for 30 minutes.

Preheat oven to 350°F (180°C).

Beat eggs and sugar in medium bowl with electric mixer until thick and pale.

Add cream cheese, rind and cranberry mixture and beat until smooth.

Pour mixture into crust and smooth top. Place on baking sheet. Bake in preheated oven for 45 to 55 minutes or until filling is just set. Mixture will set further on cooling. Cool in oven with door ajar. Filling may separate from crust a little. Cover and refrigerate for 3 hours or until cold.

Lemon Curd Topping: Stir butter, sugar and juice over medium heat until butter is melted. Remove from heat and let cool for 10 minutes.

Do-ahead tips: *Cheesecake is best made a day ahead and stored covered in refrigerator. Lemon curd can be made 3 days ahead and kept covered in refrigerator.*

Whisk in eggs until well combined. Stir over low heat for about 10 minutes or until thickened. Do not overheat mixture or it will curdle. Strain into small bowl. Cover and refrigerate, stirring occasionally, until cold. Mixture will thicken on cooling.

Spread curd evenly over top of cold cheesecake. Cover and refrigerate for 8 hours or overnight. Carefully run a knife around outer edge of cheesecake before removing ring from pan.

Chocolate Peanut Butter Fudge

You can use crunchy or smooth peanut butter for this tasty treat.

1 cup small white marshmallows

$2/3$ cup peanut butter

$1/2$ cup butter

2 cups granulated sugar

1 cup sour cream

$1/4$ cup golden corn syrup

$9^{1}/2$ oz (300 g) dark chocolate, chopped

Grease an 8 x 8 inch (20 x 20 cm) baking pan and line base and sides with parchment paper.

Heat marshmallows, peanut butter and butter in small saucepan over medium heat, stirring, for 3 to 4 minutes, until marshmallows and butter are melted.

Combine sugar, sour cream and syrup in medium saucepan. Stir on medium-low heat until sugar is dissolved. Increase heat to high and bring to boil then immediately reduce heat to medium. Simmer, uncovered, stirring occasionally, until mixture reaches 220°F (110°C) on a candy thermometer. Mixture will turn a light caramel color. Remove from heat and stir for 2 minutes.

Do-ahead tips: *This dessert can be made a week ahead and stored in a sealed container in refrigerator.*

Add peanut butter mixture and chocolate and stir until melted. Immediately scrape into prepared pan; smooth top. Let stand until set. Refrigerate for 3 hours or until cold. Cut into 1 inch (2.5 cm) squares.

Refrigerate fudge or keep it in a cool, dry place.

Panforte

This traditional Italian 'fruitcake' is best made a day or two before serving and is perfect after dinner with coffee. Cut into thin wedges, it makes a lovely gift when placed into cellophane bags or gift boxes and tied with a pretty ribbon.

1 cup all purpose flour

1/3 cup cocoa powder

1/2 tsp ground cinnamon

1/2 tsp ground nutmeg

1/8 tsp salt

1 cup (7 oz/220 g) coarsely chopped glazed pineapple

1 cup (6 oz/185 g) dried figs, coarsely chopped

1 cup (6 oz/185 g) pitted dates, coarsely chopped

1/2 cup (2 1/2 oz/75 g) dried apricots, coarsely chopped

1 1/4 cups (7 oz/210 g) Brazil nuts, toasted and coarsely chopped

1 1/4 cups (6 oz/185 g) hazelnuts, toasted, peeled and coarsely chopped (see sidebar on p. 151)

2/3 cup golden corn syrup

2/3 cup granulated sugar

1/2 cup packed brown sugar

1/4 cup water

6 1/2 oz (200 g) dark chocolate, melted (see p. 6)

Grease a 9 inch (22 cm) springform pan and line base and side with 3 layers of parchment paper. Preheat oven to 325°F (160°C).

Sift flour, cocoa, cinnamon, nutmeg and salt in large bowl. Stir in dried fruits and nuts.

Heat syrup, both sugars and water in small saucepan over medium heat until sugar is dissolved. Boil gently, uncovered, without stirring, for 2 minutes. Add to fruit and nut mixture and stir until well combined.

Add chocolate and stir until well combined. Press mixture firmly into prepared pan; this task is easier if you dampen your fingers with a little water first. Bake in preheated oven for 45 to 50 minutes or until just firm. Let cool in pan completely before cutting into thin wedges.

To peel toasted hazelnuts, wrap in a clean tea towel and rub vigorously. Most of the skin will peel away.

Do-ahead tips: *Panforte can be made 1 week ahead. Store, covered, in a cool place.*

Coconut Nut Clusters

If you don't want to use foil liners or bon-bon cups, just drop the mixture onto foil-lined baking sheets.

30 small foil or paper liners, approximately

13 oz (400 g) white chocolate, melted (see p. 6)

1 cup (5 oz/155 g) macadamia nuts, toasted (see p. 7), coarsely chopped

1/2 cup (2 1/2 oz/75 g) shelled pistachio nuts, toasted (see p. 7)

1/2 cup medium unsweetened coconut, toasted (see p. 7)

melted dark chocolate for drizzling

Place cases on baking sheet.

Combine all ingredients in small bowl. Drop 2 teaspoons of mixture into each liner. Refrigerate for about 3 hours or until set.

Drizzle with melted chocolate.

Do-ahead tips: *Clusters can be made a week ahead and stored in a sealed container in the refrigerator.*

Walnut and Date Loaves

These mini loaves make a lovely addition to a festive gift basket. For extra decadence, slice and serve with butter.

1½ cups (8 oz/250 g) pitted dates, chopped

1 cup packed brown sugar

1 cup water

⅓ cup butter

1 egg, lightly beaten

2 cups all purpose flour

½ tsp baking soda

4 tsp baking powder

¼ tsp salt

⅔ cup (2½ oz/70 g) walnuts, toasted (see p. 7), coarsely chopped

icing sugar for dusting

Grease nine 2½ x 4 x 1 inch (6 x 10 x 2.5 cm) mini loaf pans.

Combine dates, sugar, water and butter in medium saucepan over medium heat until butter is melted and sugar is dissolved. Bring to boil then remove from heat; let cool.

Preheat oven to 350°F (180°C).

Add egg and stir until well combined.

Sift flour, baking powder, baking soda and salt into date mixture. Add walnuts and stir until well combined.

Spoon mixture into prepared pans until three-quarters full. Bake in preheated oven for about 30 minutes or until skewer inserted into middle of one loaf comes out clean. Let stand in pans for 10 minutes before transferring to wire rack to cool. Dust with icing sugar if desired.

Do-ahead tips: *These can be made 1 month ahead and frozen in sealed bags but are best served when fresh and still warm.*

Chocolate Caramel Squares

Wrap these as gifts or serve with coffee for a decadent treat at the end of a meal. Cut into triangles or squares.

Coconut Base

1½ cups all purpose flour

1½ cups medium unsweetened coconut

1¼ cups packed brown sugar

¾ cup butter, melted

2 tsp baking powder

⅛ tsp salt

Caramel Filling

2 x 10 fl oz (300 ml) cans sweetened condensed milk

3 Tbsp butter

3 Tbsp golden corn syrup

1 tsp vanilla

Chocolate Topping

6½ oz (200 g) dark chocolate, chopped

¼ cup butter

Grease a 9 x 13 inch (23 x 32.5 cm) baking pan and line base and sides with parchment paper, ensuring parchment paper comes 1 inch (2.5 cm) over long sides of pan. Preheat oven to 350°F (180°C).

Coconut Base: Combine all ingredients in large bowl. Press mixture over bottom of prepared pan. Bake in preheated oven for about 15 minutes until golden and brown around edges.

Caramel Filling: Stir all ingredients in medium saucepan over medium-low heat until butter is melted. Stir

Do-ahead tips: *These squares can be made 3 days ahead and stored in a sealed container in refrigerator. Let stand at room temperature for 30 minutes before serving.*

constantly for about 10 minutes or until mixture is slightly thickened, taking care not to burn mixture.

Pour filling over hot base and spread until smooth. Bake for about 10 minutes or until bubbling and lightly brown around edges; cool.

Chocolate Topping: Stir chocolate and butter in small saucepan over low heat for about 2 minutes or until chocolate is almost melted. Remove from heat and stir until smooth.

Spread warm topping over filling. Let stand at room temperature until cool. Cover and refrigerate for about 3 hours until cold. Holding the edges of the parchment paper, lift from pan. Cut into 32 squares or 64 triangles.

Drinks

Pear and Cranberry Warmer

Makes about 12 cups.

Apple juice can be used as a substitute for pear juice.

- 8 cups cranberry juice
- 4 cups pear juice
- 3 medium pears, peeled and chopped
- 2/3 cup small cranberries (fresh or frozen)
- 2 x 5 inch (13 cm) pieces orange peel
- 2 cinnamon sticks
- 10 whole cloves

Combine all ingredients in a slow cooker. Heat, covered, on low for 8 to 10 hours or on high for 4 to 5 hours. Remove peel, cinnamon sticks and cloves before serving. Keep warm.

Hot Chocolate

Makes about 5 cups.

To make this kid friendly, omit the liqueur.

- 3 cups milk
- 1/2 cup half and half (10% MF)
- 9 oz (300 g) dark chocolate, chopped
- 1/4 tsp ground cinnamon
- 3/4 cup coffee flavored liqueur (e.g., Kahlua) (optional)
- 1 cup whipping cream

instant hot chocolate mix for garnish

Heat milk and half and half in medium saucepan over medium-high heat until bubbling. Remove from heat and add chocolate; stir until melted. Add cinnamon and liqueur (if using) and stir until well combined. Heat mixture over medium heat until hot but not boiling.

Meanwhile, beat whipping cream, using electric mixer, until soft peaks form. Pour hot chocolate into warmed cups, top with whipped cream and sprinkle with chocolate mix.

Mulled Wine

Makes about 7 cups.

- 2 x 750 ml bottles pinot noir or merlot
- 1 cup port
- 1/2 cup (4 oz/125 g) crystallized ginger, chopped
- 2 cinnamon sticks
- 6 whole cloves
- 5 cardamom pods, bruised (see p. 7)
- 1 medium orange, sliced
- 2/3 cup packed brown sugar

Combine all ingredients in slow cooker. Heat, covered,

on low for 8 to 10 hours or on high for 4 to 5 hours. Remove cinnamon sticks, cloves and cardamom pods before serving. Keep warm.

Pineapple and Strawberry Cocktail

Makes about 5 cups.

- 2 cups pineapple juice
- ½ cup vodka
- ½ cup orange-flavored liqueur (e.g., Cointreau)
- 2 cups frozen strawberries
- 1 Tbsp lime juice

Place all ingredients in blender and process until smooth.

Eggnog

Makes about 4½ cups.

- 6 egg yolks
- ½ cup granulated sugar
- 2 cups half and half (10% MF)
- ½ tsp ground nutmeg
- ⅛ tsp ground cinnamon
- ⅔ cup spiced rum

extra ground nutmeg for sprinkling

Whisk yolks and sugar in medium bowl until sugar is dissolved. Heat cream in medium saucepan until bubbles appear around side of pan. Gradually whisk hot cream into egg mixture. Pour mixture back into saucepan and add spices. Stir constantly over medium-low heat until mixture coats the back of a spoon. Remove from heat and stir in rum.

Sprinkle individual servings with extra nutmeg if desired.

Peach Lime Daiquiris

Makes about 3½ cups.

- 12½ oz (398 ml) can peaches in light syrup, undrained
- ½ cup white rum
- ⅓ cup orange-flavored liqueur (e.g., Cointreau)
- ½ cup lime juice
- 1 cup ice cubes

Place all ingredients in blender and process until smooth.

Index